THE GLASS MENAGERIE *was first produced by Eddie Dowling and Louis J. Singer at the Civic Theatre, Chicago, Ill., on December 26, 1944, and at the Playhouse Theatre, New York City, on March 31, 1945, with the following cast:*

THE MOTHER	Laurette Taylor
HER SON	Eddie Dowling
HER DAUGHTER	Julie Haydon
THE GENTLEMAN CALLER	Anthony Ross

SETTING DESIGNED AND LIGHTED by Jo Mielziner
ORIGINAL MUSIC COMPOSED by Paul Bowles
STAGED by Eddie Dowling and Margo Jones

THE GLASS MENAGERIE

BY TENNESSEE WILLIAMS

PLAYS

Baby Doll (a screenplay)
Cat on a Hot Tin Roof
The Glass Menagerie
The Night of the Iguana
Orpheus Descending
Period of Adjustment
A Streetcar Named Desire
Suddenly Last Summer
Summer and Smoke
Three Plays
    The Rose Tattoo
    Camino Real
    Sweet Bird of Youth
27 Wagons Full of Cotton and Other Plays

POETRY

In the Winter of Cities

PROSE

The Roman Spring of Mrs. Stone
One Arm and Other Stories
Hard Candy and Other Stories

The Glass Menagerie

Tennessee Williams

Nobody, not even the rain, has such small hands.

E. E. CUMMINGS

THE NEW CLASSICS

NEW DIRECTIONS

THE CHARACTERS

AMANDA WINGFIELD (*the mother*)...........Laurette Taylor
   A little woman of great but confused vitality clinging frantically to another time and place. Her characterization must be carefully created, not copied from type. She is not paranoiac, but her life is paranoia. There is much to admire in Amanda, and as much to love and pity as there is to laugh at. Certainly she has endurance and a kind of heroism, and though her foolishness makes her unwittingly cruel at times, there is tenderness in her slight person.

LAURA WINGFIELD (*her daughter*).............Julie Haydon
   Amanda, having failed to establish contact with reality, continues to live vitally in her illusions, but Laura's situation is even graver. A childhood illness has left her crippled, one leg slightly shorter than the other, and held in a brace. This defect need not be more than suggested on the stage. Stemming from this, Laura's separation increases till she is like a piece of her own glass collection, too exquisitely fragile to move from the shelf.

TOM WINGFIELD (*her son*)..................Eddie Dowling
   And the narrator of the play. A poet with a job in a warehouse. His nature is not remorseless, but to escape from a trap he has to act without pity.

JIM O'CONNOR (*the gentleman caller*).........Anthony Ross
   A nice, ordinary, young man.

SCENE

AN ALLEY IN ST. LOUIS

PART I. Preparation for a Gentleman Caller.

PART II. The Gentleman calls.

Time: Now and the Past.

PRODUCTION NOTES

Being a "memory play," *The Glass Menagerie* can be presented with unusual freedom of convention. Because of its considerably delicate or tenuous material, atmospheric touches and subtleties of direction play a particularly important part. Expressionism and all other unconventional techniques in drama have only one valid aim, and that is a closer approach to truth. When a play employs unconventional techniques, it is not, or certainly shouldn't be, trying to escape its responsibility of dealing with reality, or interpreting experience, but is actually or should be attempting to find a closer approach, a more penetrating and vivid expression of things as they are. The straight realistic play with its genuine frigidaire and authentic ice-cubes, its characters that speak exactly as its audience speaks, corresponds to the academic landscape and has the same virtue of a photographic likeness. Everyone should know nowadays the unimportance of the photographic in art: that truth, life, or reality is an organic thing which the poetic imagination can represent or suggest, in essence, only through transformation, through changing into other forms than those which were merely present in appearance.

These remarks are not meant as a preface only to this particular play. They have to do with a conception of a new, plastic theatre which must take the place of the exhausted theatre of realistic conventions if the theatre is to resume vitality as a part of our culture.

PRODUCTION NOTES

THE SCREEN DEVICE

There is *only one important difference between the original and acting version of the play* and that is the *omission* in the latter of the device which I tentatively included in my *original* script. This device was the use of a screen on which were projected magic-lantern slides bearing images or titles. I do not regret the omission of this device from the present Broadway production. The extraordinary power of Miss Taylor's performance made it suitable to have the utmost simplicity in the physical production. But I think it may be interesting to some readers to see how this device was conceived. So I am putting it into the published manuscript. These images and legends, projected from behind, were cast on a section of wall between the front-room and dining-room areas, which should be indistinguishable from the rest when not in use.

The purpose of this will probably be apparent. It is to give accent to certain values in each scene. Each scene contains a particular point (or several) which is structurally the most important. In an episodic play, such as this, the basic structure or narrative line may be obscured from the audience; the effect may seem fragmentary rather than architectural. This may not be the fault of the play so much as a lack of attention in the audience. The legend or image upon the screen will strengthen the effect of what is merely allusion in the writing and allow the primary point to be made more simply and lightly than if the entire responsibility were on the spoken lines. Aside from this structural value, I think the screen will have a definite emotional appeal, less definable but just as important. An imaginative producer or director may invent many other uses for this device than those indicated in the present script. In fact the possibilities of the device seem much larger to me than the instance of this play can possibly utilize.

THE MUSIC

Another extra-literary accent in this play is provided by the use of music. A single recurring tune, "The Glass Menagerie," is used to give emotional emphasis to suitable passages. This tune is like circus music, not when you are on the grounds or in the immediate vicinity of the parade, but when you are at some distance and very likely thinking of something else. It seems under those circumstances to continue almost interminably and it weaves in and out of your preoccupied consciousness; then it is the lightest, most delicate music in the world and perhaps the saddest. It expresses the surface vivacity of life with the underlying strain of immutable and inexpressible sorrow. When you look at a piece of delicately spun glass you think of two things: how beautiful it is and how easily it can be broken. Both of those ideas should be woven into the recurring tune, which dips in and out of the play as if it were carried on a wind that changes. It serves as a thread of connection and allusion between the narrator with his separate point in time and space and the subject of his story. Between each episode it returns as reference to the emotion, nostalgia, which is the first condition of the play. It is primarily Laura's music and therefore comes out most clearly when the play focuses upon her and the lovely fragility of glass which is her image.

THE LIGHTING

The lighting in the play is not realistic. In keeping with the atmosphere of memory, the stage is dim. Shafts of light are focused on selected areas or actors, sometimes in contradistinction to what is the apparent center. For instance, in the quarrel scene between Tom and Amanda, in which Laura has no active part, the clearest pool of light is on her figure. This is also true of the supper scene, when her silent figure on the sofa should remain the visual center. The light upon Laura should be distinct from the others, having a peculiar pristine clarity such as light used in early religious portraits of female saints or madonnas. A certain correspondence to light in religious paintings, such as El Greco's, where the figures are radiant in atmosphere that is relatively dusky, could be effectively used throughout the play. (It will also permit a more effective use of the screen.) A free, imaginative use of light can be of enormous value in giving a mobile, plastic quality to plays of a more or less static nature.

T. W.

THE CATASTROPHE OF SUCCESS

[This essay was first published in "The New York Times," later reprinted in "Story" and is now included, as an introduction, in The New Classics edition of this play.]

THIS winter marked the third anniversary of the Chicago opening of "The Glass Menagerie," an event which terminated one part of my life and began another about as different in all external circumstances as could well be imagined. I was snatched out of virtual oblivion and thrust into sudden prominence, and from the precarious tenancy of furnished rooms about the country I was removed to a suite in a first-class Manhattan hotel. My experience was not unique. Success has often come that abruptly into the lives of Americans. The Cinderella story is our favorite national myth, the cornerstone of the film industry if not of the Democracy itself. I have seen it enacted on the screen so often that I was now inclined to yawn at it, not with disbelief but with an attitude of Who Cares! Anyone with such beautiful teeth and hair as the screen protagonist of such a story was bound to have a good time one way or another, and you could bet your bottom dollar and all the tea in China that that one would not be caught dead or alive at any meeting involving a social conscience.

No, my experience was not exceptional, but neither was it quite ordinary, and if you are willing to accept the somewhat eclectic proposition that I had not been writing with such an experience in mind—and many people are not willing to believe that a playwright is interested in anything but popular success—there may be some point in comparing the two estates.

The sort of life which I had had previous to this popular success was one that required endurance, a life of clawing and scratching along a sheer surface and holding on tight with raw fingers to every inch of rock higher than the one caught hold of before, but it was a good life because it was the sort of life for which the human organism is created.

I was not aware of how much vital energy had gone into this struggle until the struggle was removed. I was out on a level plateau with my arm still thrashing and my lungs still grabbing at air that no longer resisted. This was security at last.

I sat down and looked about me and was suddenly very depressed. I thought to myself, this is just a period of adjustment. Tomorrow morning I will wake up in this first-class hotel suite above the discreet hum of an East Side boulevard and I will appreciate its elegance and luxuriate in its comforts and know that I have arrived at our American plan of Olympus. Tomorrow morning when I look at the green satin sofa I will fall in love with it. It is only temporarily that the green satin looks like slime on stagnant water.

But in the morning the inoffensive little sofa looked more revolting than the night before and I was already getting too fat for the $125 suit which a fashionable acquaintance had selected for me. In the suite things began to break accidentally. An arm came off the sofa. Cigarette burns appeared on the polished surface of the furniture. Windows were left open and a rain storm flooded the suite. But the maid always put it straight and the patience of the management was inexhaustible. Late parties could not offend them seriously. Nothing short of a demolition bomb seemed to bother my neighbors.

I lived on room service. But in this, too, there was a disenchantment. Some time between the moment when I ordered dinner over the phone and when it was rolled into my living room like a corpse on a rubber-wheeled table, I lost all interest in it. Once I ordered a sirloin steak and a chocolate sundae, but everything was so cunningly disguised on the table that I mistook the chocolate sauce for gravy and poured it over the sirloin steak.

Of course all this was the more trivial aspect of a spiritual dislocation that began to manifest itself in far more disturbing ways. I soon found myself becoming indifferent to people. A well of cynicism rose in me. Conversations all sounded as if they had been recorded years ago and were being played back on a turn-table. Sincerity and kindliness seemed to have gone out of my friends' voices. I suspected them of hypocrisy. I stopped calling them, stopped seeing them. I was impatient of what I took to be inane flattery.

I got so sick of hearing people say, "I loved your play!" that I could not say thank you any more. I choked on the words and turned rudely away from the usually sincere person. I no longer felt any pride in the play itself but began to dislike it, probably because I felt too lifeless inside ever to create another. I was walking around dead in my shoes and I knew it but there were no friends I knew or trusted sufficiently, at that time, to take them aside and tell them what was the matter.

This curious condition persisted about three months, till late spring, when I decided to have another eye operation mainly because of the excuse it gave me to withdraw from the world behind a gauze mask. It was my fourth eye operation, and perhaps I should explain that I had been afflicted for about five years with a cataract on my left eye which required a series of needling operations and finally an operation on the muscle of the eye. (The eye is still in my head. So much for that.)

Well, the gauze mask served a purpose. While I was resting in the hospital the friends whom I had neglected or affronted in one way or another began to call on me and now that I was in pain and darkness, their voices seemed to have changed, or rather that unpleasant mutation which I had suspected earlier in the season had now disappeared and they sounded now as they had used to sound in the lamented days of my obscurity. Once more they were sincere and kindly voices with the ring of truth in them and that quality of understanding for which I had originally sought them out.

As far as my physical vision was concerned, this last operation was only relatively successful (although it left me with an apparently clear black pupil in the right position, or nearly so) but in another, figurative way, it had served a much deeper purpose.

When the gauze mask was removed I found myself in a readjusted world. I checked out of the handsome suite at the first-class hotel, packed my papers and a few incidental belongings and left for Mexico, an elemental country where you can quickly forget the false dignities and conceits imposed by success, a country where vagrants innocent as children curl up to sleep on the pavements and human voices, especially when their language is not familiar to the ear, are soft as birds'. My public self, that artifice of mirrors, did not exist here and so my natural being was resumed.

Then, as a final act of restoration, I settled for a while at Chapala to work on a play called "The Poker Night," which later became "A Streetcar Named Desire." It is only in his work that an artist can find reality and satisfaction, for the actual world is less intense than the world of his invention and consequently his life, without recourse to violent disorder, does not seem very substantial. The right condition for him is that

xvi

in which his work is not only convenient but unavoidable.

For me a convenient place to work is a remote place among strangers where there is good swimming. But life should require a certain minimal effort. You should not have too many people waiting on you, you should have to do most things for yourself. Hotel service is embarrassing. Maids, waiters, bellhops, porters and so forth are the most embarrassing people in the world for they continually remind you of inequities which we accept as the proper thing. The sight of an ancient woman, gasping and wheezing as she drags a heavy pail of water down a hotel corridor to mop up the mess of some drunken overprivileged guest, is one that sickens and weighs upon the heart and withers it with shame for this world in which it is not only tolerated but regarded as proof positive that the wheels of Democracy are functioning as they should without interference from above or below. Nobody should have to clean up anybody else's mess in this world. It is terribly bad for both parties, but probably worse for the one receiving the service.

I have been corrupted as much as anyone else by the vast number of menial services which our society has grown to expect and depend on. We should do for ourselves or let the machines do for us, the glorious technology that is supposed to be the new light of the world. We are like a man who has bought a great amount of equipment for a camping trip, who has the canoe and the tent and the fishing lines and the axe and the guns, the mackinaw and the blankets, but who now, when all the preparations and the provisions are piled expertly together, is suddenly too timid to set out on the journey but remains where he was yesterday and the day before and the day before that, looking suspiciously through white lace curtains at the clear sky he distrusts. Our great technology is a God-given chance for adventure and for progress which we are afraid to attempt. Our ideas and our ideals remain exactly what they were and where they were three centuries ago. No. I beg your pardon. It is no longer safe for a man to even declare them!

This is a long excursion from a small theme into a large one which I did not intend to make, so let me go back to what I was saying before.

This is an over-simplification. One does not escape that easily from the seduction of an effete way of life. You cannot arbitrarily say to yourself, I will now continue my life as it was before this thing, Success, happened to me. But once you fully apprehend the vacuity of a life without struggle you are equipped with the basic means of salvation. Once you know this is true, that the heart of man, his body and his brain, are forged in a white-hot furnace for the purpose of conflict (the struggle of creation) and that with the conflict removed, the man is a sword cutting daisies, that not privation but luxury is the wolf at the door and that the fangs of this wolf are all the little vanities and conceits and laxities that Success is heir to —why, then with this knowledge you are at least in a position of knowing where danger lies.

You know, then, that the public Somebody you are when you "have a name" is a fiction created with mirrors and that the only somebody worth being is the solitary and unseen you that existed from your first breath and which is the sum of your actions and so is constantly in a state of becoming under your own volition—and knowing these things, you can even survive the catastrophe of Success!

It is never altogether too late, unless you embrace the Bitch Goddess, as William James called her, with both arms and find in her smothering caresses exactly what the homesick little boy in you always wanted, absolute protection and utter effort-

xviii

lessness. Security is a kind of death, I think, and it can come to you in a storm of royalty checks beside a kidney-shaped pool in Beverly Hills or anywhere at all that is removed from the conditions that made you an artist, if that's what you are or were or intended to be. Ask anyone who has experienced the kind of success I am talking about— What good is it? Perhaps to get an honest answer you will have to give him a shot of truth-serum but the word he will finally groan is unprintable in genteel publications.

Then what is good? The obsessive interest in human affairs, plus a certain amount of compassion and moral conviction, that first made the experience of living something that must be translated into pigment or music or bodily movement or poetry or prose or anything that's dynamic and expressive—that's what's good for you if you're at all serious in your aims. William Saroyan wrote a great play on this theme, that purity of heart is the one success worth having. "In the time of your life— live!" That time is short and it doesn't return again. It is slipping away while I write this and while you read it, and the monosyllable of the clock is Loss, loss, loss, unless you devote your heart to its opposition.

THE GLASS MENAGERIE

SCENE I

The Wingfield apartment is in the rear of the building, one of those vast hive-like conglomerations of cellular living-units that flower as warty growths in overcrowded urban centers of lower middle-class population and are symptomatic of the impulse of this largest and fundamentally enslaved section of American society to avoid fluidity and differentiation and to exist and function as one interfused mass of automatism.

The apartment faces an alley and is entered by a fire-escape, a structure whose name is a touch of accidental poetic truth, for all of these huge buildings are always burning with the slow and implacable fires of human desperation. The fire-escape is included in the set—that is, the landing of it and steps descending from it.

The scene is memory and is therefore nonrealistic. Memory takes a lot of poetic license. It omits some details; others are exaggerated, according to the emotional value of the articles it touches, for memory is seated predominantly in the heart. The interior is therefore rather dim and poetic.

At the rise of the curtain, the audience is faced with the dark, grim rear wall of the Wingfield tenement. This building, which runs parallel to the footlights, is flanked on both sides by dark, narrow alleys which run into murky canyons of tangled clotheslines, garbage cans and the sinister latticework of neighboring fire-escapes. It is up and down these side alleys that exterior entrances and exits are made, during the play. At the end of TOM's *opening commentary, the dark*

3

tenement wall slowly reveals (by means of a transparency) the interior of the ground floor Wingfield apartment.

Downstage is the living room, which also serves as a sleeping room for LAURA, *the sofa unfolding to make her bed. Upstage, center, and divided by a wide arch or second proscenium with transparent faded portieres (or second curtain), is the dining room. In an old-fashioned what-not in the living room are seen scores of transparent glass animals. A blown-up photograph of the father hangs on the wall of the living room, facing the audience, to the left of the archway. It is the face of a very handsome young man in a doughboy's First World War cap. He is gallantly smiling, ineluctably smiling, as if to say, "I will be smiling forever."*

The audience hears and sees the opening scene in the dining room through both the transparent fourth wall of the building and the transparent gauze portieres of the dining-room arch. It is during this revealing scene that the fourth wall slowly ascends, out of sight. This transparent exterior wall is not brought down again until the very end of the play, during TOM's *final speech.*

The narrator is an undisguised convention of the play. He takes whatever license with dramatic convention as is convenient to his purposes.

TOM *enters dressed as a merchant sailor from alley, stage left, and strolls across the front of the stage to the fire-escape. There he stops and lights a cigarette. He addresses the audience.*

TOM

Yes, I have tricks in my pocket, I have things up my sleeve. But I am the opposite of a stage magician. He gives you illusion that has the appearance of truth. I give you truth in the pleasant disguise of illusion.

4

To begin with, I turn back time. I reverse it to that quaint period, the thirties, when the huge middle class of America was matriculating in a school for the blind. Their eyes had failed them, or they had failed their eyes, and so they were having their fingers pressed forcibly down on the fiery Braille alphabet of a dissolving economy.

In Spain there was revolution. Here there was only shouting and confusion.

In Spain there was Guernica. Here there were disturbances of labor, sometimes pretty violent, in otherwise peaceful cities such as Chicago, Cleveland, Saint Louis . . .

This is the social background of the play.

(MUSIC.)

The play is memory.

Being a memory play, it is dimly lighted, it is sentimental, it is not realistic.

In memory everything seems to happen to music. That explains the fiddle in the wings.

I am the narrator of the play, and also a character in it.

The other characters are my mother, Amanda, my sister, Laura, and a gentleman caller who appears in the final scenes.

He is the most realistic character in the play, being an emissary from a world of reality that we were somehow set apart from.

But since I have a poet's weakness for symbols, I am using this character also as a symbol; he is the long delayed but always expected something that we live for.

There is a fifth character in the play who doesn't appear except in this larger-than-life-size photograph over the mantel.

This is our father who left us a long time ago.

He was a telephone man who fell in love with long distances; he gave up his job with the telephone company and skipped the light fantastic out of town . . .

The last we heard of him was a picture post-card from Mazatlan, on the Pacific coast of Mexico, containing a message of two words—

"Hello— Good-bye!" and no address.

I think the rest of the play will explain itself. . . .

(AMANDA's *voice becomes audible through the portieres.*)

(LEGEND ON SCREEN: "OU SONT LES NEIGES.")

(*He divides the portieres and enters the upstage area.*)

(AMANDA *and* LAURA *are seated at a drop-leaf table. Eating is indicated by gestures without food or utensils.* AMANDA *faces the audience.* TOM *and* LAURA *are seated in profile.*)

(*The interior has lit up softly and through the scrim we see* AMANDA *and* LAURA *seated at the table in the upstage area.*)

AMANDA

(*Calling*)

Tom?

TOM

Yes, Mother.

AMANDA

We can't say grace until you come to the table!

TOM

Coming, Mother. (*He bows slightly and withdraws, reappearing a few moments later in his place at the table.*)

AMANDA

(*To her son*)

Honey, don't *push* with your *fingers*. If you have to push

6

with something, the thing to push with is a crust of bread.
And chew—chew! Animals have sections in their stomachs
which enable them to digest food without mastication, but
human beings are supposed to chew their food before they
swallow it down. Eat food leisurely, son, and really enjoy
it. A well-cooked meal has lots of delicate flavors that have
to be held in the mouth for appreciation. So chew your food
and give your salivary glands a chance to function!

(TOM *deliberately lays his imaginary fork down and
pushes his chair back from the table.*)

TOM

I haven't enjoyed one bite of this dinner because of your
constant directions on how to eat it. It's you that make me
rush through meals with your hawk-like attention to every
bite I take. Sickening—spoils my appetite—all this discussion
of—animals' secretion—salivary glands—mastication!

AMANDA

(*Lightly*)

Temperament like a Metropolitan star! (*He rises and
crosses downstage*) You're not excused from the table.

TOM

I'm getting a cigarette.

AMANDA

You smoke too much.

(LAURA *rises.*)

LAURA

I'll bring in the blanc mange.

(*He remains standing with his cigarette by the portieres during the following.*)

7

AMANDA

(*Rising*)

No, sister, no, sister—you be the lady this time and I'll be the darky.

LAURA

I'm already up.

AMANDA

Resume your seat, little sister—I want you to stay fresh and pretty—for gentlemen callers!

LAURA

I'm not expecting any gentlemen callers.

AMANDA

(*Crossing out to kitchenette. Airily*)

Sometimes they come when they are least expected! Why, I remember one Sunday afternoon in Blue Mountain— (*Enters kitchenette.*)

TOM

I know what's coming!

LAURA

Yes. But let her tell it.

TOM

Again?

LAURA

She loves to tell it.

(AMANDA *returns with bowl of dessert.*)

AMANDA

One Sunday afternoon in Blue Mountain—your mother received—*seventeen!*—gentlemen callers! Why, sometimes there weren't chairs enough to accommodate them all. We

8

had to send the nigger over to bring in folding chairs from the parish house.

TOM

(*Remaining at portieres*)

How did you entertain those gentlemen callers?

AMANDA

I understood the art of conversation!

TOM

I bet you could talk.

AMANDA

Girls in those days *knew* how to talk, I can tell you.

TOM

Yes?

(IMAGE: AMANDA AS A GIRL ON A PORCH, GREETING CALL-ERS.)

AMANDA

They knew how to entertain their gentlemen callers. It wasn't enough for a girl to be possessed of a pretty face and a graceful figure—although I wasn't slighted in either respect. She also needed to have a nimble wit and a tongue to meet all occasions.

TOM

What did you talk about?

AMANDA

Things of importance going on in the world! Never anything coarse or common or vulgar. (*She addresses* TOM *as though he were seated in the vacant chair at the table though he remains by portieres. He plays this scene as though he held the book*) My callers were gentlemen—all! Among my callers were some of the most prominent young planters of the Mississippi Delta—planters and sons of planters!

(TOM *motions for music and a spot of light on* AMANDA.)

(*Her eyes lift, her face glows, her voice becomes rich and elegiac.*)

(SCREEN LEGEND: "OU SONT LES NEIGES.")

There was young Champ Laughlin who later became vice-president of the Delta Planters Bank.

Hadley Stevenson who was drowned in Moon Lake and left his widow one hundred and fifty thousand in Government bonds.

There were the Cutrere brothers, Wesley and Bates. Bates was one of my bright particular beaux! He got in a quarrel with that wild Wainwright boy. They shot it out on the floor of Moon Lake Casino. Bates was shot through the stomach. Died in the ambulance on his way to Memphis. His widow was also well-provided for, came into eight or ten thousand acres, that's all. She married him on the rebound—never loved her—carried my picture on him the night he died!

And there was that boy that every girl in the Delta had set her cap for! That beautiful, brilliant young Fitzhugh boy from Greene County!

TOM

What did he leave his widow?

AMANDA

He never married! Gracious, you talk as though all of my old admirers had turned up their toes to the daisies!

TOM

Isn't this the first you've mentioned that still survives?

AMANDA

That Fitzhugh boy went North and made a fortune—came to be known as the Wolf of Wall Street! He had the Midas touch, whatever he touched turned to gold!

And I could have been Mrs. Duncan J. Fitzhugh, mind you! But—I picked your *father!*

LAURA

(*Rising*)

Mother, let me clear the table.

AMANDA

No, dear, you go in front and study your typewriter chart. Or practice your shorthand a little. Stay fresh and pretty!— It's almost time for our gentlemen callers to start arriving. (*She flounces girlishly toward the kitchenette*) How many do you suppose we're going to entertain this afternoon?

(TOM *throws down the paper and jumps up with a groan.*)

LAURA

(*Alone in the dining room*)

I don't believe we're going to receive any, Mother.

AMANDA

(*Reappearing, airily*)

What? No one—not one? You must be joking! (LAURA *nervously echoes her laugh. She slips in a fugitive manner through the half-open portieres and draws them gently behind her. A shaft of very clear light is thrown on her face against the faded tapestry of the curtains.* MUSIC: "THE GLASS MENAGERIE" UNDER FAINTLY. *Lightly*) Not one gentleman caller? It can't be true! There must be a flood, there must have been a tornado!

LAURA

It isn't a flood, it's not a tornado, Mother. I'm just not popular like you were in Blue Mountain. . . . (TOM *utters another groan.* LAURA *glances at him with a faint, apologetic smile. Her voice catching a little*) Mother's afraid I'm going to be an old maid.

THE SCENE DIMS OUT WITH "GLASS MENAGERIE" MUSIC

SCENE II

"Laura, Haven't You Ever Liked Some Boy?"
On the dark stage the screen is lighted with the image of blue roses.

Gradually LAURA's *figure becomes apparent and the screen goes out.*

The music subsides.

LAURA *is seated in the delicate ivory chair at the small claw-foot table.*

She wears a dress of soft violet material for a kimono—her hair tied back from her forehead with a ribbon.

She is washing and polishing her collection of glass.

AMANDA *appears on the fire-escape steps. At the sound of her ascent,* LAURA *catches her breath, thrusts the bowl of ornaments away and seats herself stiffly before the diagram of the typewriter keyboard as though it held her spellbound.*

Something has happened to AMANDA. *It is written in her face as she climbs to the landing: a look that is grim and hopeless and a little absurd.*

She has on one of those cheap or imitation velvety-looking cloth coats with imitation fur collar. Her hat is five or six years old, one of those dreadful cloche hats that were worn in the late twenties and she is clasping an enormous black patent-leather pocketbook with nickel clasps and initials. This is her full-dress outfit, the one she usually wears to the D.A.R.

Before entering she looks through the door.

She purses her lips, opens her eyes very wide, rolls them upward and shakes her head.

Then she slowly lets herself in the door. Seeing her mother's expression LAURA *touches her lips with a nervous gesture.*

LAURA

Hello, Mother, I was— (*She makes a nervous gesture toward the chart on the wall.* AMANDA *leans against the shut door and stares at* LAURA *with a martyred look.*)

AMANDA

Deception? Deception? (*She slowly removes her hat and gloves, continuing the sweet suffering stare. She lets the hat and gloves fall on the floor—a bit of acting.*)

LAURA

(*Shakily*)

How was the D.A.R. meeting? (AMANDA *slowly opens her purse and removes a dainty white handkerchief which she shakes out delicately and delicately touches to her lips and nostrils*) Didn't you go to the D.A.R. meeting, Mother?

AMANDA

(*Faintly, almost inaudibly*)

—No.—No. (*Then more forcibly*) I did not have the strength—to go to the D.A.R. In fact, I did not have the courage! I wanted to find a hole in the ground and hide myself in it forever! (*She crosses slowly to the wall and removes the diagram of the typewriter keyboard. She holds it in front of her for a second, staring at it sweetly and sorrowfully—then bites her lips and tears it in two pieces.*)

LAURA

(*Faintly*)

Why did you do that, Mother? (AMANDA *repeats the same procedure with the chart of the Gregg Alphabet*) Why are you—

AMANDA

Why? Why? How old are you, Laura?

LAURA

Mother, you know my age.

AMANDA

I thought that you were an adult; it seems that I was mistaken. (*She crosses slowly to the sofa and sinks down and stares at* LAURA.)

LAURA

Please don't stare at me, Mother.

(AMANDA *closes her eyes and lowers her head. Count ten.*)

AMANDA

What are we going to do, what is going to become of us, what is the future?

(*Count ten.*)

LAURA

Has something happened, Mother? (AMANDA *draws a long breath and takes out the handkerchief again. Dabbing process*) Mother, has—something happened?

AMANDA

I'll be all right in a minute, I'm just bewildered—(*Count five*)—by life. . . .

LAURA

Mother, I wish that you would tell me what's happened!

AMANDA

As you know, I was supposed to be inducted into my office at the D.A.R. this afternoon. (IMAGE: A SWARM OF TYPEWRITERS) But I stopped off at Rubicam's business college to speak

15

to your teachers about your having a cold and ask them what progress they thought you were making down there.

LAURA

Oh. . . .

AMANDA

I went to the typing instructor and introduced myself as your mother. She didn't know who you were. Wingfield, she said. We don't have any such student enrolled at the school!

I assured her she did, that you had been going to classes since early in January.

"I wonder," she said, "if you could be talking about that terribly shy little girl who dropped out of school after only a few days' attendance?"

"No," I said, "Laura, my daughter, has been going to school every day for the past six weeks!"

"Excuse me," she said. She took the attendance book out and there was your name, unmistakably printed, and all the dates you were absent until they decided that you had dropped out of school.

I still said, "No, there must have been some mistake! There must have been some mix-up in the records!"

And she said, "No—I remember her perfectly now. Her hands shook so that she couldn't hit the right keys! The first time we gave a speed-test, she broke down completely—was sick at the stomach and almost had to be carried into the wash-room! After that morning she never showed up any more. We phoned the house but never got any answer—while I was working at Famous and Barr, I suppose, demonstrating those— Oh!"

I felt so weak I could barely keep on my feet!

I had to sit down while they got me a glass of water!

Fifty dollars' tuition, all of our plans—my hopes and ambitions for you—just gone up the spout, just gone up the spout like that.

> (LAURA *draws a long breath and gets awkwardly to her feet. She crosses to the victrola and winds it up.*)

What are you doing?

LAURA

Oh! (*She releases the handle and returns to her seat.*)

AMANDA

Laura, where have you been going when you've gone out pretending that you were going to business college?

LAURA

I've just been going out walking.

AMANDA

That's not true.

LAURA

It is. I just went walking.

AMANDA

Walking? Walking? In winter? Deliberately courting pneumonia in that light coat? Where did you walk to, Laura?

LAURA

All sorts of places—mostly in the park.

AMANDA

Even after you'd started catching that cold?

LAURA

It was the lesser of two evils, Mother. (IMAGE: WINTER

SCENE IN PARK) I couldn't go back up. I—threw up—on the floor!

AMANDA

From half past seven till after five every day you mean to tell me you walked around in the park, because you wanted to make me think that you were still going to Rubicam's Business College?

LAURA

It wasn't as bad as it sounds. I went inside places to get warmed up.

AMANDA

Inside where?

LAURA

I went in the art museum and the bird-houses at the Zoo. I visited the penguins every day! Sometimes I did without lunch and went to the movies. Lately I've been spending most of my afternoons in the Jewel-box, that big glass house where they raise the tropical flowers.

AMANDA

You did all this to deceive me, just for deception? (LAURA *looks down*) Why?

LAURA

Mother, when you're disappointed, you get that awful suffering look on your face, like the picture of Jesus' mother in the museum!

AMANDA

Hush!

LAURA

I couldn't face it.

(*Pause. A whisper of strings.*)
(LEGEND: "THE CRUST OF HUMILITY.")

THE GLASS MENAGERIE

AMANDA

(*Hopelessly fingering the huge pocketbook*)
So what are we going to do the rest of our lives? Stay home and watch the parades go by? Amuse ourselves with the glass menagerie, darling? Eternally play those worn-out phonograph records your father left as a painful reminder of him?

We won't have a business career—we've given that up because it gave us nervous indigestion! (*Laughs wearily*) What is there left but dependency all our lives? I know so well what becomes of unmarried women who aren't prepared to occupy a position. I've seen such pitiful cases in the South— barely tolerated spinsters living upon the grudging patronage of sister's husband or brother's wife!—stuck away in some little mouse-trap of a room—encouraged by one in-law to visit another—little birdlike women without any nest—eating the crust of humility all their life!

Is that the future that we've mapped out for ourselves?

I swear it's the only alternative I can think of!

It isn't a very pleasant alternative, is it?

Of course—some girls *do marry*.

(LAURA *twists her hands nervously.*)
Haven't you ever liked some boy?

LAURA

Yes. I liked one once. (*Rises*) I came across his picture a while ago.

AMANDA

(*With some interest*)
He gave you his picture?

LAURA

No, it's in the year-book.

AMANDA
(*Disappointed*)

Oh—a high-school boy.

(SCREEN IMAGE: JIM AS HIGH-SCHOOL HERO BEARING A SILVER CUP.)

LAURA

Yes. His name was Jim. (LAURA *lifts the heavy annual from the claw-foot table*) Here he is in *The Pirates of Penzance*.

AMANDA
(*Absently*)

The what?

LAURA

The operetta the senior class put on. He had a wonderful voice and we sat across the aisle from each other Mondays, Wednesdays and Fridays in the Aud. Here he is with the silver cup for debating! See his grin?

AMANDA
(*Absently*)

He must have had a jolly disposition.

LAURA

He used to call me—Blue Roses.

(IMAGE: BLUE ROSES.)

AMANDA

Why did he call you such a name as that?

LAURA

When I had that attack of pleurosis—he asked me what was the matter when I came back. I said pleurosis—he thought that I said Blue Roses! So that's what he always called me after that. Whenever he saw me, he'd holler,

"Hello, Blue Roses!" I didn't care for the girl that he went out with. Emily Meisenbach. Emily was the best-dressed girl at Soldan. She never struck me, though, as being sincere . . . It says in the Personal Section—they're engaged. That's—six years ago! They must be married by now.

AMANDA

Girls that aren't cut out for business careers usually wind up married to some nice man. (*Gets up with a spark of revival*) Sister, that's what you'll do!
    (LAURA *utters a startled, doubtful laugh. She reaches quickly for a piece of glass.*)

LAURA

But, Mother—

AMANDA

Yes? (*Crossing to photograph.*)

LAURA

    (*In a tone of frightened apology*)
I'm—crippled!
    (IMAGE: SCREEN.)

AMANDA

Nonsense! Laura, I've told you never, never to use that word. Why, you're not crippled, you just have a little defect—hardly noticeable, even! When people have some slight disadvantage like that, they cultivate other things to make up for it—develop charm—and vivacity—and—*charm!* That's all you have to do! (*She turns again to the photograph*) One thing your father had *plenty of*—was *charm!*
    (TOM *motions to the fiddle in the wings.*)

THE SCENE FADES OUT WITH MUSIC

SCENE III

LEGEND ON SCREEN: "AFTER THE FIASCO—"

TOM *speaks from the fire-escape landing.*

TOM

After the fiasco at Rubicam's Business College, the idea of getting a gentleman caller for Laura began to play a more and more important part in Mother's calculations.

It became an obsession. Like some archetype of the universal unconscious, the image of the gentleman caller haunted our small apartment. . . .

(IMAGE: YOUNG MAN AT DOOR WITH FLOWERS.)

An evening at home rarely passed without some allusion to this image, this spectre, this hope. . . .

Even when he wasn't mentioned, his presence hung in Mother's preoccupied look and in my sister's frightened, apologetic manner—hung like a sentence passed upon the Wingfields!

Mother was a woman of action as well as words.

She began to take logical steps in the planned direction.

Late that winter and in the early spring—realizing that extra money would be needed to properly feather the nest and plume the bird—she conducted a vigorous campaign on the telephone, roping in subscribers to one of those magazines for matrons called *The Home-maker's Companion,* the type of journal that features the serialized sublimations of ladies of letters who think in terms of delicate cup-like breasts, slim, tapering waists, rich, creamy thighs, eyes like wood-smoke in

22

autumn, fingers that soothe and caress like strains of music, bodies as powerful as Etruscan sculpture.

(SCREEN IMAGE: GLAMOR MAGAZINE COVER.)

(AMANDA *enters with phone on long extension cord. She is spotted in the dim stage.*)

AMANDA

Ida Scott? This is Amanda Wingfield!

We *missed* you at the D.A.R. last Monday!

I said to myself: She's probably suffering with that sinus condition! How is that sinus condition?

Horrors! Heaven have mercy!—You're a Christian martyr, yes, that's what you are, a Christian martyr!

Well, I just now happened to notice that your subscription to the *Companion's* about to expire! Yes, it expires with the next issue, honey!—just when that wonderful new serial by Bessie Mae Hopper is getting off to such an exciting start. Oh, honey, it's something that you can't miss! You remember how *Gone With the Wind* took everybody by storm? You simply couldn't go out if you hadn't read it. All everybody *talked* was Scarlett O'Hara. Well, this is a book that critics already compare to *Gone With the Wind*. It's the *Gone With the Wind* of the post-World War generation!—What?— Burning?—Oh, honey, don't let them burn, go take a look in the oven and I'll hold the wire! Heavens—I think she's hung up!

DIM OUT

(LEGEND ON SCREEN: "YOU THINK I'M IN LOVE WITH CON-TINENTAL SHOEMAKERS?")

(*Before the stage is lighted, the violent voices of* TOM *and* AMANDA *are heard.*)

(*They are quarreling behind the portieres. In front of*

23

them stands LAURA *with clenched hands and panicky expression*.)

(*A clear pool of light on her figure throughout this scene.*)

TOM

What in Christ's name am I—

AMANDA

(*Shrilly*)

Don't you use that—

TOM

Supposed to do!

AMANDA

Expression! Not in my—

TOM

Ohhh!

AMANDA

Presence! Have you gone out of your senses?

TOM

I have, that's true, *driven* out!

AMANDA

What is the matter with you, you—big—big—IDIOT!

TOM

Look!—I've got *no thing,* no single thing—

AMANDA

Lower your voice!

TOM

In my life here that I can call my OWN! Everything is—

24

AMANDA

Stop that shouting!

TOM

Yesterday you confiscated my books! You had the nerve, to—

AMANDA

I took that horrible novel back to the library—yes! That hideous book by that insane Mr. Lawrence. (TOM *laughs wildly*) I cannot control the output of diseased minds or people who cater to them— (TOM *laughs still more wildly*) BUT I WON'T ALLOW SUCH FILTH BROUGHT INTO MY HOUSE! No, no, no, no, no!

TOM

House, house! Who pays rent on it, who makes a slave of himself to—

AMANDA

(*Fairly screeching*)

Don't you DARE to—

TOM

No, no, *I* mustn't say things! *I've* got to just—

AMANDA

Let me tell you—

TOM

I don't want to hear any more! (*He tears the portieres open. The upstage area is lit with a turgid smoky red glow.*)
(AMANDA's *hair is in metal curlers and she wears a very old bathrobe, much too large for her slight figure, a relic of the faithless Mr. Wingfield.*)
(*An upright typewriter and a wild disarray of manuscripts is on the drop-leaf table. The quarrel was prob-*

ably precipitated by AMANDA's *interruption of his cre-
ative labor. A chair lying overthrown on the floor.)*
*(Their gesticulating shadows are cast on the ceiling by
the fiery glow.)*

AMANDA

You *will* hear more, you—

TOM

No, I won't hear more, I'm going out!

AMANDA

You come right back in—

TOM

Out, out, out! Because I'm—

AMANDA

Come back here, Tom Wingfield! I'm not through talking
to you!

TOM

Oh, go—

LAURA

(Desperately)

—Tom!

AMANDA

You're going to listen, and no more insolence from you!
I'm at the end of my patience!
(He comes back toward her.)

TOM

What do you think I'm at? Aren't I supposed to have any
patience to reach the end of, Mother? I know, I know. It
seems unimportant to you, what I'm *doing*—what I *want* to

26

do—having a little *difference* between them! You don't think that—

AMANDA

I think you've been doing things that you're ashamed of. That's why you act like this. I don't believe that you go every night to the movies. Nobody goes to the movies night after night. Nobody in their right minds goes to the movies as often as you pretend to. People don't go to the movies at nearly midnight, and movies don't let out at two A.M. Come in stumbling. Muttering to yourself like a maniac! You get three hours' sleep and then go to work. Oh, I can picture the way you're doing down there. Moping, doping, because you're in no condition.

TOM

(*Wildly*)

No, I'm in no condition!

AMANDA

What right have you got to jeopardize your job? Jeopardize the security of us all? How do you think we'd manage if you were—

TOM

Listen! You think I'm crazy *about* the *warehouse*? (*He bends fiercely toward her slight figure*) You think I'm in love with the Continental Shoemakers? You think I want to spend fifty-five *years* down there in that—*celotex interior!* with—*fluorescent—tubes!* Look! I'd rather somebody picked up a crowbar and battered out my brains—than go back mornings! I *go!* Every time you come in yelling that God damn *"Rise and Shine!" "Rise and Shine!"* I say to myself, "How *lucky dead* people are!" But I get up. I *go!* For sixty-five dollars a month I give up all that I dream of doing and being *ever!*

And you say self—*self's* all I ever think of. Why, listen, if self is what I thought of, Mother, I'd be where he is—GONE! (*Pointing to father's picture*) As far as the system of transportation reaches! (*He starts past her. She grabs his arm*) Don't grab at me, Mother!

AMANDA

Where are you going?

TOM

I'm going to the *movies!*

AMANDA

I don't believe that lie!

TOM

(*Crouching toward her, overtowering her tiny figure She backs away, gasping*)

I'm going to opium dens! Yes, opium dens, dens of vice and criminals' hang-outs, Mother. I've joined the Hogan gang, I'm a hired assassin, I carry a tommy-gun in a violin case! I run a string of cat-houses in the Valley! They call me Killer, Killer Wingfield, I'm leading a double-life, a simple, honest warehouse worker by day, by night a dynamic *czar* of the *underworld, Mother.* I go to gambling casinos, I spin away fortunes on the roulette table! I wear a patch over one eye and a false mustache, sometimes I put on green whiskers. On those occasions they call me—*El Diablo!* Oh, I could tell you things to make you sleepless! My enemies plan to dynamite this place. They're going to blow us all sky-high some night! I'll be glad, very happy, and so will you! You'll go up, up on a broomstick, over Blue Mountain with seventeen gentlemen callers! You ugly—babbling old—*witch.* . . . (*He goes through a series of violent, clumsy movements, seizing his overcoat, lunging to the door, pulling it fiercely open. The women watch him, aghast. His arm catches in the sleeve of the coat as he struggles to pull it on. For a moment he is pinioned by the bulky garment. With an outraged groan he tears the coat off again, splitting the shoulder of it, and hurls it across the room. It strikes against the shelf of* LAURA's *glass collection, there is a tinkle of shattering glass.* LAURA *cries out as if wounded.*)

(MUSIC. LEGEND: "THE GLASS MENAGERIE.")

LAURA
(Shrilly)
My glass!—menagerie. . . . (*She covers her face and turns away.*)

(*But* AMANDA *is still stunned and stupefied by the "ugly witch" so that she barely notices this occurrence. Now she recovers her speech.*)

AMANDA
(*In an awful voice*)
I won't speak to you—until you apologize! (*She crosses through portieres and draws them together behind her.* TOM *is left with* LAURA. LAURA *clings weakly to the mantel with her face averted.* TOM *stares at her stupidly for a moment. Then he crosses to shelf. Drops awkwardly on his knees to collect the fallen glass, glancing at* LAURA *as if he would speak but couldn't.*)
"*The Glass Menagerie*" *steals in as*

THE SCENE DIMS OUT

SCENE IV

The interior is dark. Faint light in the alley.

A deep-voiced bell in a church is tolling the hour of five as the scene commences.

TOM *appears at the top of the alley. After each solemn boom of the bell in the tower, he shakes a little noise-maker or rattle as if to express the tiny spasm of man in contrast to the sustained power and dignity of the Almighty. This and the unsteadiness of his advance make it evident that he has been drinking.*

As he climbs the few steps to the fire-escape landing light steals up inside. LAURA *appears in night-dress, observing* TOM's *empty bed in the front room.*

TOM *fishes in his pockets for door-key, removing a motley assortment of articles in the search, including a perfect shower of movie-ticket stubs and an empty bottle. At last he finds the key, but just as he is about to insert it, it slips from his fingers. He strikes a match and crouches below the door.*

TOM

(Bitterly)

One crack—and it falls through!

(LAURA opens the door.)

LAURA

Tom! Tom, what are you doing?

TOM

Looking for a door-key.

LAURA

Where have you been all this time?

TOM

I have been to the movies.

LAURA

All this time at the movies?

TOM

There was a very long program. There was a Garbo picture and a Mickey Mouse and a travelogue and a newsreel and a preview of coming attractions. And there was an organ solo and a collection for the milk-fund—simultaneously—which ended up in a terrible fight between a fat lady and an usher!

LAURA

(*Innocently*)

Did you have to stay through everything?

TOM

Of course! And, oh, I forgot! There was a big stage show! The headliner on this stage show was Malvolio the Magician. He performed wonderful tricks, many of them, such as pouring water back and forth between pitchers. First it turned to wine and then it turned to beer and then it turned to whiskey. I know it was whiskey it finally turned into because he needed somebody to come up out of the audience to help him, and I came up—both shows! It was Kentucky Straight Bourbon. A very generous fellow, he gave souvenirs. (*He pulls from his back pocket a shimmering rainbow-colored scarf*) He gave me this. This is his magic scarf. You can have it, Laura. You wave it over a canary cage and you get a bowl of gold-fish. You wave it over the gold-fish bowl and they fly away canaries. . . . But the wonderfullest trick of all was the coffin trick. We nailed him into a coffin and he got out of the coffin without removing one nail. (*He has come inside*) There is a trick that would come in handy for me—get me out of this 2 by 4 situation! (*Flops onto bed and starts removing shoes.*)

LAURA

Tom—Shhh!

TOM

What're you shushing me for?

LAURA

You'll wake up Mother.

TOM

Goody, goody! Pay 'er back for all those "Rise an' Shines." (*Lies down, groaning*) You know it don't take much intelligence to get yourself into a nailed-up coffin, Laura. But who in hell ever got himself out of one without removing one nail?

(*As if in answer, the father's grinning photograph lights up.*)

SCENE DIMS OUT

(*Immediately following: The church bell is heard striking six. At the sixth stroke the alarm clock goes off in* AMANDA's *room, and after a few moments we hear her calling: "Rise and Shine! Rise and Shine! Laura, go tell your brother to rise and shine!"*)

TOM

(*Sitting up slowly*)

I'll rise—but I won't shine.

(*The light increases.*)

32

AMANDA

Laura, tell your brother his coffee is ready.
(LAURA *slips into front room.*)

LAURA

Tom!—It's nearly seven. Don't make Mother nervous. (*He stares at her stupidly. Beseechingly*) Tom, speak to Mother this morning. Make up with her, apologize, speak to her!

TOM

She won't to me. It's her that started not speaking.

LAURA

If you just say you're sorry she'll start speaking.

TOM

Her not speaking—is that such a tragedy?

LAURA

Please—please!

AMANDA

(*Calling from kitchenette*)

Laura, are you going to do what I asked you to do, or do I have to get dressed and go out myself?

LAURA

Going, going—soon as I get on my coat! (*She pulls on a shapeless felt hat with nervous, jerky movement, pleadingly glancing at* TOM. *Rushes awkwardly for coat. The coat is one of* AMANDA's, *inaccurately made-over, the sleeves too short for* LAURA) Butter and what else?

AMANDA

(*Entering upstage*)

Just butter. Tell them to charge it.

LAURA

Mother, they make such faces when I do that.

AMANDA

Sticks and stones can break our bones, but the expression on Mr. Garfinkel's face won't harm us! Tell your brother his coffee is getting cold.

LAURA

(*At door*)

Do what I asked you, will you, will you, Tom?
(*He looks sullenly away.*)

AMANDA

Laura, go now or just don't go at all!

LAURA

(*Rushing out*)

Going—going! (*A second later she cries out.* TOM *springs up and crosses to door.* AMANDA *rushes anxiously in.* TOM *opens the door.*)

TOM

Laura?

LAURA

I'm all right. I slipped, but I'm all right.

AMANDA

(*Peering anxiously after her*)

If anyone breaks a leg on those fire-escape steps, the land-lord ought to be sued for every cent he possesses! (*She shuts door. Remembers she isn't speaking and returns to other room.*)

(*As* TOM *enters listlessly for his coffee, she turns her back to him and stands rigidly facing the window on the gloomy gray vault of the areaway. Its light on her face with its aged but childish features is cruelly sharp, satirical as a Daumier print.)*

(MUSIC UNDER: "AVE MARIA.")

(TOM *glances sheepishly but sullenly at her averted figure and slumps at the table. The coffee is scalding hot; he sips it and gasps and spits it back in the cup. At his gasp,* AMANDA *catches her breath and half turns. Then catches herself and turns back to window.)*

(TOM *blows on his coffee, glancing sidewise at his mother. She clears her throat.* TOM *clears his. He starts to rise. Sinks back down again, scratches his head, clears his throat again.* AMANDA *coughs.* TOM *raises his cup in both hands to blow on it, his eyes staring over the rim of it at his mother for several moments. Then he slowly sets the cup down and awkwardly and hesitantly rises from the chair.)*

TOM

(Hoarsely)

Mother. I—I apologize, Mother. (AMANDA *draws a quick, shuddering breath. Her face works grotesquely. She breaks into childlike tears*) I'm sorry for what I said, for everything that I said, I didn't mean it.

AMANDA

(Sobbingly.)

My devotion has made me a witch and so I make myself hateful to my children!

TOM

No, you don't.

AMANDA

I worry so much, don't sleep, it makes me nei vous!

TOM

(Gently)

I understand that.

AMANDA

I've had to put up a solitary battle all these years. But you're my right-hand bower! Don't fall down, don't fail!

TOM

(Gently)

I try, Mother.

AMANDA

(With great enthusiasm)

Try and you will SUCCEED! (*The notion makes her breathless.*) Why, you—you're just *full* of natural endowments! Both of my children—they're *unusual* children! Don't you think I know it? I'm so—*proud!* Happy and—feel I've—so much to be thankful for but— Promise me one thing, Son!

TOM

What, Mother?

AMANDA

Promise, son, you'll—never be a drunkard!

TOM

(Turns to her grinning)

I will never be a drunkard, Mother.

AMANDA

That's what frightened me so, that you'd be drinking! Eat a bowl of Purina!

TOM

Just coffee, Mother.

AMANDA

Shredded wheat biscuit?

TOM

No. No, Mother, just coffee.

AMANDA

You can't put in a day's work on an empty stomach. You've got ten minutes—don't gulp! Drinking too-hot liquids makes cancer of the stomach. . . . Put cream in.

TOM

No, thank you.

AMANDA

To cool it.

TOM

No! No, thank you, I want it black.

AMANDA

I know, but it's not good for you. We have to do all that we can to build ourselves up. In these trying times we live in, all that we have to cling to is—each other. . . . That's why it's so important to— Tom, I— I sent out your sister so I could discuss something with you. If you hadn't spoken I would have spoken to you. (*Sits down.*)

TOM

(*Gently*)

What is it, Mother, that you want to discuss?

AMANDA

Laura!

(TOM *puts his cup down slowly.*)

(LEGEND ON SCREEN: "LAURA.")

(MUSIC: "THE GLASS MENAGERIE.")

TOM

—Oh.—Laura . . .

AMANDA

(*Touching his sleeve*)

You know how Laura is. So quiet but—still water runs deep! She notices things and I think she—broods about them. (TOM *looks up*) A few days ago I came in and she was crying.

TOM

What about?

AMANDA

You.

TOM

Me?

AMANDA

She has an idea that you're not happy here.

TOM

What gave her that idea?

AMANDA

What gives her any idea? However, you do act strangely. I—I'm not criticizing, understand *that!* I know your ambitions do not lie in the warehouse, that like everybody in the whole wide world—you've had to—make sacrifices, but—Tom —Tom—life's not easy, it calls for—Spartan endurance! There's so many things in my heart that I cannot describe to you! I've never told you but I—*loved* your father. . . .

TOM

(*Gently*)

I know that, Mother.

AMANDA

And you—when I see you taking after his ways! Staying out late—and—well, you *had* been drinking the night you were in that—terrifying condition! Laura says that you hate the apartment and that you go out nights to get away from it! Is that true, Tom?

TOM

No. You say there's so much in your heart that you can't describe to me. That's true of me, too. There's so much in my heart that I can't describe to *you!* So let's respect each other's—

AMANDA

But, why—*why,* Tom—are you always so *restless?* Where do you *go* to, nights?

TOM

I—go to the movies.

AMANDA

Why do you go to the movies so much, Tom?

TOM

I go to the movies because—I like adventure. Adventure is something I don't have much of at work, so I go to the movies.

AMANDA

But, Tom, you go to the movies *entirely* too *much!*

TOM

I like a lot of adventure.

(AMANDA *looks baffled, then hurt. As the familiar inquisition resumes he becomes hard and impatient again.* AMANDA *slips back into her querulous attitude toward him.*)

(IMAGE ON SCREEN: SAILING VESSEL WITH JOLLY ROGER.)

AMANDA

Most young men find adventure in their careers.

TOM

Then most young men are not employed in a warehouse.

AMANDA

The world is full of young men employed in warehouses
and offices and factories.

TOM

Do all of them find adventure in their careers?

AMANDA

They do or they do without it! Not everybody has a craze
for adventure.

TOM

Man is by instinct a lover, a hunter, a fighter, and none
of those instincts are given much play at the warehouse!

AMANDA

Man is by instinct! Don't quote instinct to me! Instinct is
something that people have got away from! It belongs to
animals! Christian adults don't want it!

TOM

What do Christian adults want, then, Mother?

AMANDA

Superior things! Things of the mind and the spirit! Only,
animals have to satisfy instincts! Surely your aims are somewhat higher than theirs! Than monkeys—pigs—

TOM

I reckon they're not.

AMANDA

You're joking. However, that isn't what I wanted to discuss.

60

TOM
(Rising)

I haven't much time.

AMANDA
(Pushing his shoulders)

Sit down.

TOM

You want me to punch in red at the warehouse, Mother?

AMANDA

You have five minutes. I want to talk about Laura.

(LEGEND: "PLANS AND PROVISIONS.")

TOM

All right! What about Laura?

AMANDA

We have to be making some plans and provisions for her. She's older than you, two years, and nothing has happened. She just drifts along doing nothing. It frightens me terribly how she just drifts along.

TOM

I guess she's the type that people call home girls.

AMANDA

There's no such type, and if there is, it's a pity! That is unless the home is hers, with a husband!

TOM

What?

AMANDA

Oh, I can see the handwriting on the wall as plain as I see the nose in front of my face! It's terrifying!

More and more you remind me of your father! He was out all hours without explanation!—Then *left! Good-bye!*

And me with the bag to hold. I saw that letter you got from the Merchant Marine. I know what you're dreaming of. I'm not standing here blindfolded.

Very well, then. Then *do* it!

But not till there's somebody to take your place.

TOM

What do you mean?

AMANDA

I mean that as soon as Laura has got somebody to take care of her, married, a home of her own, independent—why, then you'll be free to go wherever you please, on land, on sea, whichever way the wind blows you!

But until that time you've got to look out for your sister. I don't say me because I'm old and don't matter! I say for your sister because she's young and dependent.

I put her in business college—a dismal failure! Frightened her so it made her sick at the stomach.

I took her over to the Young People's League at the church. Another fiasco. She spoke to nobody, nobody spoke to her. Now all she does is fool with those pieces of glass and play those worn-out records. What kind of a life is that for a girl to lead?

TOM

What can I do about it?

AMANDA

Overcome selfishness!

Self, self, self is all that you ever think of!

(TOM *springs up and crosses to get his coat. It is ugly and bulky. He pulls on a cap with earmuffs.*)

42

Where is your muffler? Put your wool muffler on!

(*He snatches it angrily from the closet and tosses it around his neck and pulls both ends tight.*)

Tom! I haven't said what I had in mind to ask you.

TOM

I'm too late to—

AMANDA

(*Catching his arm—very importunately. Then shyly*)

Down at the warehouse, aren't there some—nice young men?

TOM

No!

AMANDA

There *must* be—*some* . . .

TOM

Mother—

(*Gesture.*)

AMANDA

Find out one that's clean-living—doesn't drink and—ask him out for sister!

TOM

What?

AMANDA

For *sister!* To *meet!* Get *acquainted!*

TOM

(*Stamping to door*)

Oh, my *go-osh!*

AMANDA

Will you? (*He opens door. Imploringly*) Will you? (*He starts down*) Will you? *Will* you, dear?

TOM
(*Calling back*)

YES!

(AMANDA *closes the door hesitantly and with a troubled but faintly hopeful expression.*)

SCREEN IMAGE: GLAMOR MAGAZINE COVER.
Spot AMANDA *at phone.*

AMANDA

Ella Cartwright? This is Amanda Wingfield!

How are you, honey?

How is that kidney condition?

(*Count five.*)

Horrors!

(*Count five.*)

You're a Christian martyr, yes, honey, that's what you are, a Christian martyr!

Well, I just now happened to notice in my little red book that your subscription to the *Companion* has just run out! I knew that you wouldn't want to miss out on the wonderful serial starting in this new issue. It's by Bessie Mae Hopper, the first thing she's written since *Honeymoon for Three.*

Wasn't that a strange and interesting story? Well, this one is even lovelier, I believe. It has a sophisticated, society background. It's all about the horsey set on Long Island!

FADE OUT

SCENE V

LEGEND ON SCREEN: "ANNUNCIATION." *Fade with music.*
*It is early dusk of a spring evening. Supper has just been
finished in the Wingfield apartment.* AMANDA *and* LAURA *in
light-colored dresses are removing dishes from the table, in
the upstage area, which is shadowy, their movements for-
malized almost as a dance or ritual, their moving forms as
pale and silent as moths.*

TOM, *in white shirt and trousers, rises from the table and
crosses toward the fire-escape.*

> AMANDA
> (*As he passes her*)
> Son, will you do me a favor?

> TOM
> What?

> AMANDA
> Comb your hair! You look so pretty when your hair is
> combed! (TOM *slouches on sofa with evening paper. Enor-
> mous caption "Franco Triumphs"*) There is only one respect
> in which I would like you to emulate your father.

> TOM
> What respect is that?

> AMANDA
> The care he always took of his appearance. He never al-
> lowed himself to look untidy. (*He throws down the paper
> and crosses to fire-escape*) Where are you going?

45

TOM

I'm going out to smoke.

AMANDA

You smoke too much. A pack a day at fifteen cents a pack. How much would that amount to in a month? Thirty times fifteen is how much, Tom? Figure it out and you will be astounded at what you could save. Enough to give you a night-school course in accounting at Washington U! Just think what a wonderful thing that would be for you, Son!

(TOM *is unmoved by the thought.*)

TOM

I'd rather smoke. (*He steps out on landing, letting the screen door slam.*)

AMANDA

(*Sharply*)

I know! That's the tragedy of it. . . . (*Alone, she turns to look at her husband's picture.*)

(DANCE MUSIC: "ALL THE WORLD IS WAITING FOR THE SUN-RISE!")

TOM

(*To the audience*)

Across the alley from us was the Paradise Dance Hall. On evenings in spring the windows and doors were open and the music came outdoors. Sometimes the lights were turned out except for a large glass sphere that hung from the ceiling. It would turn slowly about and filter the dusk with delicate rainbow colors. Then the orchestra played a waltz or a tango, something that had a slow and sensuous rhythm. Couples would come outside, to the relative privacy of the alley. You could see them kissing behind ash-pits and telephone poles.

This was the compensation for lives that passed like mine, without any change or adventure.

Adventure and change were imminent in this year. They were waiting around the corner for all these kids.

Suspended in the mist over Berchtesgaden, caught in the folds of Chamberlain's umbrella—

In Spain there was Guernica!

But here there was only hot swing music and liquor, dance halls, bars, and movies, and sex that hung in the gloom like a chandelier and flooded the world with brief, deceptive rainbows. . . .

All the world was waiting for bombardments!

(AMANDA *turns from the picture and comes outside.*)

AMANDA
(*Sighing*)

A fire-escape landing's a poor excuse for a porch. (*She spreads a newspaper on a step and sits down, gracefully and demurely as if she were settling into a swing on a Mississippi veranda*) What are you looking at?

TOM

The moon.

AMANDA

Is there a moon this evening?

TOM

It's rising over Garfinkel's Delicatessen.

AMANDA

So it is! A little silver slipper of a moon. Have you made a wish on it yet?

TOM

Um-hum.

AMANDA

What did you wish for?

TOM

That's a secret.

AMANDA

A secret, huh? Well, I won't tell mine either. I will be just as mysterious as you.

TOM

I bet I can guess what yours is.

AMANDA

Is my head so transparent?

TOM

You're not a sphinx.

AMANDA

No, I don't have secrets. I'll tell you what I wished for on the moon. Success and happiness for my precious children! I wish for that whenever there's a moon, and when there isn't a moon, I wish for it, too.

TOM

I thought perhaps you wished for a gentleman caller.

AMANDA

Why do you say that?

TOM

Don't you remember asking me to fetch one?

AMANDA

I remember suggesting that it would be nice for your sister if you brought home some nice young man from the warehouse. I think that I've made that suggestion more than once.

TOM

Yes, you have made it repeatedly.

AMANDA

Well?

TOM

We are going to have one.

AMANDA

What?

TOM

A gentleman caller!

   (THE ANNUNCIATION IS CELEBRATED WITH MUSIC.)
   (AMANDA *rises.*)
   (IMAGE ON SCREEN: CALLER WITH BOUQUET.)

AMANDA

You mean you have asked some nice young man to come over?

TOM

Yep. I've asked him to dinner.

AMANDA

You really did?

TOM

I did!

AMANDA

You did, and did he—*accept?*

TOM

He did!

AMANDA

Well, well—well, well! That's—lovely!

49

TOM

I thought that you would be pleased.

AMANDA

It's definite, then?

TOM

Very definite.

AMANDA

Soon?

TOM

Very soon.

AMANDA

For heaven's sake, stop putting on and tell me some things, will you?

TOM

What things do you want me to tell you?

AMANDA

Naturally I would like to know when he's *coming!*

TOM

He's coming tomorrow.

AMANDA

Tomorrow?

TOM

Yep. Tomorrow.

AMANDA

But, Tom!

TOM

Yes, Mother?

AMANDA

Tomorrow gives me no time!

TOM

Time for what?

AMANDA

Preparations! Why didn't you phone me at once, as soon as you asked him, the minute that he accepted? Then, don't you see, I could have been getting ready!

TOM

You don't have to make any fuss.

AMANDA

Oh, Tom, Tom, Tom, of course I have to make a fuss! I want things nice, not sloppy! Not thrown together. I'll certainly have to do some fast thinking, won't I?

TOM

I don't see why you have to think at all.

AMANDA

You just don't know. We can't have a gentleman caller in a pig-sty! All my wedding silver has to be polished, the monogrammed table linen ought to be laundered! The windows have to be washed and fresh curtains put up. And how about clothes? We have to *wear* something, don't we?

TOM

Mother, this boy is no one to make a fuss over!

AMANDA

Do you realize he's the first young man we've introduced to your sister?

It's terrible, dreadful, disgraceful that poor little sister has never received a single gentleman caller! Tom, come inside! (*She opens the screen door.*)

TOM

What for?

AMANDA

I want to ask you some things.

TOM

If you're going to make such a fuss, I'll call it off, I'll tell him not to come!

AMANDA

You certainly won't do anything of the kind. Nothing offends people worse than broken engagements. It simply means I'll have to work like a Turk! We won't be brilliant, but we will pass inspection. Come on inside. (TOM *follows, groaning*) Sit down.

TOM

Any particular place you would like me to sit?

AMANDA

Thank heavens I've got that new sofa! I'm also making payments on a floor lamp I'll have sent out! And put the chintz covers on, they'll brighten things up! Of course I'd hoped to have these walls re-papered. . . . What is the young man's name?

TOM

His name is O'Connor.

AMANDA

That, of course, means fish—tomorrow is Friday! I'll have that salmon loaf—with Durkee's dressing! What does he do? He works at the warehouse?

TOM

Of course! How else would I—

AMANDA

Tom, he—doesn't drink?

TOM

Why do you ask me that?

AMANDA

Your father *did!*

TOM

Don't get started on that!

AMANDA

He *does* drink, then?

TOM

Not that I know of!

AMANDA

Make sure, be certain! The last thing I want for my daughter's a boy who drinks!

TOM

Aren't you being a little bit premature? Mr. O'Connor has not yet appeared on the scene!

AMANDA

But will tomorrow. To meet your sister, and what do I know about his character? Nothing! Old maids are better off than wives of drunkards!

TOM

Oh, my God!

AMANDA

Be still!

TOM

(*Leaning forward to whisper*)

Lots of fellows meet girls whom they don't marry!

AMANDA

Oh, talk sensibly, Tom—and don't be sarcastic! (*She has gotten a hairbrush.*)

TOM

What are you doing?

AMANDA

I'm brushing that cow-lick down!
What is this young man's position at the warehouse?

TOM

(*Submitting grimly to the brush and the interrogation*)
This young man's position is that of a shipping clerk, Mother.

AMANDA

Sounds to me like a fairly responsible job, the sort of a job *you* would be in if you just had more *get-up*.
What is his salary? Have you any idea?

TOM

I would judge it to be approximately eighty-five dollars a month.

AMANDA

Well—not princely, but—

TOM

Twenty more than I make.

AMANDA

Yes, how well I know! But for a family man, eighty-five dollars a month is not much more than you can just get by on. . . .

TOM

Yes, but Mr. O'Connor is not a family man.

54

AMANDA

He might be, mightn't he? Some time in the future?

TOM

I see. Plans and provisions.

AMANDA

You are the only young man that I know of who ignores the fact that the future becomes the present, the present the past, and the past turns into everlasting regret if you don't plan for it!

TOM

I will think that over and see what I can make of it.

AMANDA

Don't be supercilious with your mother! Tell me some more about this—what do you call him?

TOM

James D. O'Connor. The D. is for Delaney.

AMANDA

Irish on *both* sides! *Gracious!* And doesn't drink?

TOM

Shall I call him up and ask him right this minute?

AMANDA

The only way to find out about those things is to make discreet inquiries at the proper moment. When I was a girl in Blue Mountain and it was suspected that a young man drank, the girl whose attentions he had been receiving, if any girl *was*, would sometimes speak to the minister of his church, or rather her father would if her father was living, and sort of feel him out on the young man's character. That is the way such things are discreetly handled to keep a young woman from making a tragic mistake!

TOM

Then how did you happen to make a tragic mistake?

AMANDA

That innocent look of your father's had everyone fooled! He *smiled*—the world was *enchanted!*

No girl can do worse than put herself at the mercy of a handsome appearance!

I hope that Mr. O'Connor is not too good-looking.

TOM

No, he's not too good-looking. He s covered with freckles and hasn't too much of a nose.

AMANDA

He's not right-down homely, though?

TOM

Not right-down homely. Just medium homely, I'd say.

AMANDA

Character's what to look for in a man.

TOM

That's what I've always said, Mother.

AMANDA

You've never said anything of the kind and I suspect you would never give it a thought.

TOM

Don't be so suspicious of me.

56

AMANDA

At least I hope he's the type that's up and coming.

TOM

I think he really goes in for self-improvement.

AMANDA

What reason have you to think so?

TOM

He goes to night school.

AMANDA

(*Beaming*)

Splendid! What does he do, I mean study?

TOM

Radio engineering and public speaking!

AMANDA

Then he has visions of being advanced in the world!

Any young man who studies public speaking is aiming to have an executive job some day!

And radio engineering? A thing for the future!

Both of these facts are very illuminating. Those are the sort of things that a mother should know concerning any young man who comes to call on her daughter. Seriously or—not.

TOM

One little warning. He doesn't know about Laura. I didn't let on that we had dark ulterior motives. I just said, why don't you come and have dinner with us? He said okay and that was the whole conversation.

AMANDA

I bet it was! You're eloquent as an oyster.

However, he'll know about Laura when he gets here. When he sees how lovely and sweet and pretty she is, he'll thank his lucky stars he was asked to dinner.

TOM

Mother, you mustn't expect too much of Laura.

AMANDA

What do you mean?

TOM

Laura seems all those things to you and me because she's ours and we love her. We don't even notice she's crippled any more.

AMANDA

Don't say crippled! You know that I never allow that word to be used!

TOM

But face facts, Mother. She is and—that's not all—

AMANDA

What do you mean "not all"?

TOM

Laura is very different from other girls.

AMANDA

I think the difference is all to her advantage.

TOM

Not quite all—in the eyes of others—strangers—she's terribly shy and lives in a world of her own and those things make her seem a little peculiar to people outside the house.

AMANDA

Don't say peculiar.

58

TOM

Face the facts. She is.

(THE DANCE-HALL MUSIC CHANGES TO A TANGO THAT HAS A MINOR AND SOMEWHAT OMINOUS TONE.)

AMANDA

In what way is she peculiar—may I ask?

TOM
(Gently)

She lives in a world of her own—a world of—little glass ornaments, Mother. . . . (*Gets up.* AMANDA *remains holding brush, looking at him, troubled*) She plays old phonograph records and—that's about all— (*He glances at himself in the mirror and crosses to door.*)

AMANDA
(Sharply)

Where are you going?

TOM

I'm going to the movies. (*Out screen door.*)

AMANDA

Not to the movies, every night to the movies! (*Follows quickly to screen door*) I don't believe you always go to the movies! (*He is gone.* AMANDA *looks worriedly after him for a moment. Then vitality and optimism return and she turns from the door. Crossing to portieres*) Laura! Laura! (LAURA *answers from kitchenette.*)

LAURA

Yes, Mother.

AMANDA

Let those dishes go and come in front! (LAURA *appears with*

59

dish towel. Gaily) Laura, come here and make a wish on the
moon!

(SCREEN IMAGE: MOON.)

LAURA
(*Entering*)

Moon—moon?

AMANDA

A little silver slipper of a moon.

Look over your left shoulder, Laura, and make a wish!
(LAURA *looks faintly puzzled as if called out of sleep.*
AMANDA *seizes her shoulders and turns her at an angle
by the door.*)

Now!

Now, darling, *wish!*

LAURA

What shall I wish for, Mother?

AMANDA
(*Her voice trembling and her eyes suddenly filling
with tears*)

Happiness! Good fortune!
(*The violin rises and the stage dims out.*)

CURTAIN

SCENE VI

IMAGE: HIGH SCHOOL HERO.

And so the following evening I brought Jim home to dinner. I had known Jim slightly in high school. In high school Jim was a hero. He had tremendous Irish good nature and vitality with the scrubbed and polished look of white chinaware. He seemed to move in a continual spotlight. He was a star in basketball, captain of the debating club, president of the senior class and the glee club and he sang the male lead in the annual light operas. He was always running or bounding, never just walking. He seemed always at the point of defeating the law of gravity. He was shooting with such velocity through his adolescence that you would logically expect him to arrive at nothing short of the White House by the time he was thirty. But Jim apparently ran into more interference after his graduation from Soldan. His speed had definitely slowed. Six years after he left high school he was holding a job that wasn't much better than mine.

(IMAGE: CLERK.)

He was the only one at the warehouse with whom I was on friendly terms. I was valuable to him as someone who could remember his former glory, who had seen him win basketball games and the silver cup in debating. He knew of my secret practice of retiring to a cabinet of the wash-room to work on poems when business was slack in the warehouse. He called me Shakespeare. And while the other boys in the warehouse regarded me with suspicious hostility, Jim took a humorous attitude toward me. Gradually his attitude affected the others, their hostility wore off and they also began to smile at me as people smile at an oddly fashioned dog who trots across their path at some distance.

I knew that Jim and Laura had known each other at Soldan, and I had heard Laura speak admiringly of his voice. I didn't know if Jim remembered her or not. In high school Laura had been as unobtrusive as Jim had been astonishing. If he did remember Laura, it was not as my sister, for when I asked him to dinner, he grinned and said, "You know, Shakespeare, I never thought of you as having folks!"

He was about to discover that I did. . . .

(LIGHT UP STAGE.)

(LEGEND ON SCREEN: "THE ACCENT OF A COMING FOOT.")

(*Friday evening. It is about five o'clock of a late spring evening which comes "scattering poems in the sky."*)

(*A delicate lemony light is in the Wingfield apartment.*)

(AMANDA *has worked like a Turk in preparation for the gentleman caller. The results are astonishing. The new floor lamp with its rose-silk shade is in place, a colored paper lantern conceals the broken light fixture in the ceiling, new billowing white curtains are at the windows, chintz covers are on chairs and sofa, a pair of new sofa pillows make their initial appearance.*)

(*Open boxes and tissue paper are scattered on the floor.*)

(LAURA *stands in the middle with lifted arms while* AMANDA *crouches before her, adjusting the hem of the new dress, devout and ritualistic. The dress is colored and designed by memory. The arrangement of* LAURA'S *hair is changed; it is softer and more becoming. A fragile, unearthly prettiness has come out in* LAURA: *she is*

*like a piece of translucent glass touched by light, given
a momentary radiance, not actual, not lasting.)*

AMANDA

(Impatiently)

Why are you trembling?

LAURA

Mother, you've made me so nervous!

AMANDA

How have I made you nervous?

LAURA

By all this fuss! You make it seem so important!

AMANDA

I don't understand you, Laura. You couldn't be satisfied
with just sitting home, and yet whenever I try to arrange
something for you, you seem to resist it.

(She gets up.)

Now take a look at yourself.

No, wait! Wait just a moment—I have an idea!

LAURA

What is it now?

*(AMANDA produces two powder puffs which she wraps
in handkerchiefs and stuffs in LAURA's bosom.)*

LAURA

Mother, what are you doing?

AMANDA

They call them "Gay Deceivers"!

LAURA

I won't wear them!

AMANDA

You will!

LAURA

Why should I?

AMANDA

Because, to be painfully honest, your chest is flat.

LAURA

You make it seem like we were setting a trap.

AMANDA

All pretty girls are a trap, a pretty trap, and men expect them to be.

(LEGEND: "A PRETTY TRAP.")

Now look at yourself, young lady. This is the prettiest you will ever be!

I've got to fix myself now! You're going to be surprised by your mother's appearance! (*She crosses through portieres, humming gaily.*)

(LAURA *moves slowly to the long mirror and stares solemnly at herself.*)

(*A wind blows the white curtains inward in a slow, graceful motion and with a faint, sorrowful sighing.*)

AMANDA

(*Off stage*)

It isn't dark enough yet. (*She turns slowly before the mirror with a troubled look.*)

(LEGEND ON SCREEN: "THIS IS MY SISTER: CELEBRATE HER WITH STRINGS!" MUSIC.)

64

AMANDA

(Laughing, off)

I'm going to show you something. I'm going to make a spectacular appearance!

LAURA

What is it, Mother?

AMANDA

Possess your soul in patience—you will see!

Something I've resurrected from that old trunk! Styles haven't changed so terribly much after all. . . .

(She parts the portieres.)

Now just look at your mother!

(She wears a girlish frock of yellowed voile with a blue silk sash. She carries a bunch of jonquils—the legend of her youth is nearly revived. Feverishly.)

This is the dress in which I led the cotillion. Won the cakewalk twice at Sunset Hill, wore one spring to the Governor's ball in Jackson!

See how I sashayed around the ballroom, Laura?

(She raises her skirt and does a mincing step around the room.)

I wore it on Sundays for my gentlemen callers! I had it on the day I met your father—

I had malaria fever all that spring. The change of climate from East Tennessee to the Delta—weakened resistance—I had a little temperature all the time—not enough to be serious—just enough to make me restless and giddy!—Invitations poured in—parties all over the Delta!—"Stay in bed," said Mother, "you have fever!"—but I just wouldn't.—I took quinine but kept on going, going!—Evenings, dances!—Afternoons, long, long rides! Picnics—lovely!—So lovely, that

65

country in May.—All lacy with dogwood, literally flooded with jonquils!—That was the spring I had the craze for jonquils. Jonquils became an absolute obsession. Mother said, "Honey, there's no more room for jonquils." And still I kept on bringing in more jonquils. Whenever, wherever I saw them, I'd say, "Stop! Stop! I see jonquils!" I made the young men help me gather the jonquils! It was a joke, Amanda and her jonquils! Finally there were no more vases to hold them, every available space was filled with jonquils. No vases to hold them? All right, I'll hold them myself! And then I— (*She stops in front of the picture.* MUSIC) met your father!

Malaria fever and jonquils and then—this—boy. . . .

> (*She switches on the rose-colored lamp.*)

I hope they get here before it starts to rain.

> (*She crosses upstage and places the jonquils in bowl on table.*)

I gave your brother a little extra change so he and Mr. O'Connor could take the service car home.

LAURA

(*With altered look*)

What did you say his name was?

AMANDA

O'Connor.

LAURA

What is his first name?

AMANDA

I don't remember. Oh, yes, I do. It was—Jim!

> (LAURA *sways slightly and catches hold of a chair.*)
> (LEGEND ON SCREEN: "NOT JIM!")

LAURA

(*Faintly*)

Not—Jim!

AMANDA

Yes, that was it, it was Jim! I've never known a Jim that wasn't nice!

(MUSIC: OMINOUS.)

LAURA

Are you sure his name is Jim O'Connor?

AMANDA

Yes. Why?

LAURA

Is he the one that Tom used to know in high school?

AMANDA

He didn't say so. I think he just got to know him at the warehouse.

LAURA

There was a Jim O'Connor we both knew in high school— (*Then, with effort*) If that is the one that Tom is bringing to dinner—you'll have to excuse me, I won't come to the table.

AMANDA

What sort of nonsense is this?

LAURA

You asked me once if I'd ever liked a boy. Don't you remember I showed you this boy's picture?

AMANDA

You mean the boy you showed me in the year book?

LAURA

Yes, that boy.

AMANDA

Laura, Laura, were you in love with that boy?

LAURA

I don't know, Mother. All I know is I couldn't sit at the table if it was him!

AMANDA

It won't be him! It isn't the least bit likely. But whether it is or not, you will come to the table. You will not be excused.

LAURA

I'll have to be, Mother.

AMANDA

I don't intend to humor your silliness, Laura. I've had too much from you and your brother, both!

So just sit down and compose yourself till they come. Tom has forgotten his key so you'll have to let them in, when they arrive.

LAURA

(*Panicky*)

Oh, Mother—*you* answer the door!

AMANDA

(*Lightly*)

I'll be in the kitchen—busy!

LAURA

Oh, Mother, please answer the door, don't make me do it!

AMANDA

(*Crossing into kitchenette*)

I've got to fix the dressing for the salmon. Fuss, fuss—silliness!—over a gentleman caller!

68

(*Door swings shut.* LAURA *is left alone.*)

(LEGEND: "TERROR!")

(*She utters a low moan and turns off the lamp—sits stiffly on the edge of the sofa, knotting her fingers together.*)

(LEGEND ON SCREEN: "THE OPENING OF A DOOR!")

(TOM *and* JIM *appear on the fire-escape steps and climb to landing. Hearing their approach,* LAURA *rises with a panicky gesture. She retreats to the portieres.*)

(*The doorbell.* LAURA *catches her breath and touches her throat. Low drums.*)

AMANDA

(*Calling*)

Laura, sweetheart! The door!

(LAURA *stares at it without moving.*)

JIM

I think we just beat the rain.

TOM

Uh-huh. (*He rings again, nervously.* JIM *whistles and fishes for a cigarette.*)

AMANDA

(*Very, very gaily*)

Laura, that is your brother and Mr. O'Connor! Will you let them in, darling?

(LAURA *crosses toward kitchenette door.*)

LAURA

(*Breathlessly*)

Mother—you go to the door!

(AMANDA *steps out of kitchenette and stares furiously at* LAURA. *She points imperiously at the door.*)

LAURA

Please, please!

AMANDA
(*In a fierce whisper*)
What is the matter with you, you silly thing?

LAURA
(*Desperately*)
Please, you answer it, *please!*

AMANDA
I told you I wasn't going to humor you, Laura. Why have you chosen this moment to lose your mind?

LAURA
Please, please, please, you go!

AMANDA
You'll have to go to the door because I can't!

LAURA
(*Despairingly*)
I can't either!

AMANDA
Why?

LAURA
I'm *sick!*

AMANDA
I'm sick, too—of your nonsense! Why can't you and your brother be normal people? Fantastic whims and behavior!
(TOM *gives a long ring.*)
Preposterous goings on! Can you give me one reason— (*Calls out lyrically*) COMING! JUST ONE SECOND!—why you should be afraid to open a door? Now you answer it, Laura!

70

LAURA

Oh, oh, oh . . . (*She returns through the portieres. Darts to the victrola and winds it frantically and turns it on.*)

AMANDA

Laura Wingfield, you march right to that door!

LAURA

Yes—yes, Mother!

(*A faraway, scratchy rendition of "Dardanella" softens the air and gives her strength to move through it. She slips to the door and draws it cautiously open.*)

(TOM *enters with the caller,* JIM O'CONNOR.)

TOM

Laura, this is Jim. Jim, this is my sister, Laura.

JIM

(*Stepping inside*)

I didn't know that Shakespeare had a sister!

LAURA

(*Retreating stiff and trembling from the door*)

How—how do you do?

JIM

(*Heartily extending his hand*)

Okay!

(LAURA *touches it hesitantly with hers.*)

JIM

Your hand's *cold*, Laura!

LAURA

Yes, well—I've been playing the victrola. . . .

71

JIM

Must have been playing classical music on it! You ought
to play a little hot swing music to warm you up!

LAURA

Excuse me—I haven't finished playing the victrola. . . .
(*She turns awkwardly and hurries into the front room. She
pauses a second by the victrola. Then catches her breath and
darts through the portieres like a frightened deer.*)

JIM
(*Grinning*)

What was the matter?

TOM

Oh—with Laura? Laura is—terribly shy.

JIM

Shy, huh? It's unusual to meet a shy girl nowadays. I don't
believe you ever mentioned you had a sister.

TOM

Well, now you know. I have one. Here is the *Post Dispatch*.
You want a piece of it?

JIM

Uh-huh.

TOM

What piece? The comics?

JIM

Sports! (*Glances at it*) Ole Dizzy Dean is on his bad
behavior.

72

TOM

(Disinterest)

Yeah? (*Lights cigarette and crosses back to fire-escape door.*)

JIM

Where are *you* going?

TOM

I'm going out on the terrace.

JIM

(Goes after him)

You know, Shakespeare—I'm going to sell you a bill of goods!

TOM

What goods?

JIM

A course I'm taking.

TOM

Huh?

JIM

In public speaking! You and me, we're not the warehouse type.

TOM

Thanks—that's good news.

But what has public speaking got to do with it?

JIM

It fits you for—executive positions!

TOM

Awww.

73

JIM

I tell you it's done a helluva lot for me.
(IMAGE: EXECUTIVE AT DESK.)

TOM

In what respect?

JIM

In every! Ask yourself what is the difference between you an' me and men in the office down front? Brains?—No!—Ability?—No! Then what? Just one little thing—

TOM

What is that one little thing?

JIM

Primarily it amounts to—social poise! Being able to square up to people and hold your own on any social level!

AMANDA
(Off stage)

Tom?

TOM

Yes, Mother?

AMANDA

Is that you and Mr. O'Connor?

TOM

Yes, Mother.

AMANDA

Well, you just make yourselves comfortable in there.

TOM

Yes, Mother.

AMANDA

Ask Mr. O'Connor if he would like to wash his hands.

74

JIM

Aw, no—no—thank you—I took care of that at the warehouse. Tom—

TOM

Yes?

JIM

Mr. Mendoza was speaking to me about you.

TOM

Favorably?

JIM

What do you think?

TOM

Well—

JIM

You're going to be out of a job if you don't wake up.

TOM

I am waking up—

JIM

You show no signs.

TOM

The signs are interior.

(IMAGE ON SCREEN: THE SAILING VESSEL WITH JOLLY ROGER AGAIN.)

TOM

I'm planning to change. (*He leans over the rail speaking with quiet exhilaration. The incandescent marquees and signs of the first-run movie houses light his face from across the alley. He looks like a voyager*) I'm right at the point of committing myself to a future that doesn't include the warehouse and Mr. Mendoza or even a night-school course in public speaking.

75

JIM

What are you gassing about?

TOM

I'm tired of the movies.

JIM

Movies!

TOM

Yes, movies! Look at them— (*A wave toward the marvels of Grand Avenue*) All of those glamorous people—having adventures—hogging it all, gobbling the whole thing up! You know what happens? People go to the *movies* instead of *moving!* Hollywood characters are supposed to have all the adventures for everybody in America, while everybody in America sits in a dark room and watches them have them! Yes, until there's a war. That's when adventure becomes available to the masses! *Everyone's* dish, not only Gable's! Then the people in the dark room come out of the dark room to have some adventures themselves—Goody, goody!—It's our turn now, to go to the South Sea Island—to make a safari— to be exotic, far-off!—But I'm not patient. I don't want to wait till then. I'm tired of the *movies* and I am *about* to *move!*

JIM
(*Incredulously*)

Move?

TOM

Yes.

JIM

When?

TOM

Soon!

76

JIM

Where? Where?

(THEME THREE MUSIC SEEMS TO ANSWER THE QUESTION, WHILE TOM THINKS IT OVER. HE SEARCHES AMONG HIS POCKETS.)

TOM

I'm starting to boil inside. I know I seem dreamy, but inside—well, I'm boiling!—Whenever I pick up a shoe, I shudder a little thinking how short life is and what I am doing!—Whatever that means, I know it doesn't mean shoes—except as something to wear on a traveler's feet! (*Finds paper*) Look—

JIM

What?

TOM

I'm a member.

JIM

(*Reading*)

The Union of Merchant Seamen.

TOM

I paid my dues this month, instead of the light bill.

JIM

You will regret it when they turn the lights off.

TOM

I won't be here.

JIM

How about your mother?

TOM

I'm like my father. The bastard son of a bastard! See how he grins? And he's been absent going on sixteen years!

JIM

You're just talking, you drip. How does your mother feel about it?

TOM

Shhh!—Here comes Mother! Mother is not acquainted with my plans!

AMANDA

(Enters portieres)

Where are you all?

TOM

On the terrace, Mother.

(They start inside. She advances to them. TOM is distinctly shocked at her appearance. Even JIM blinks a little. He is making his first contact with girlish Southern vivacity and in spite of the night-school course in public speaking is somewhat thrown off the beam by the unexpected outlay of social charm.)

(Certain responses are attempted by JIM but are swept aside by AMANDA's gay laughter and chatter. TOM is embarrassed but after the first shock JIM reacts very warmly. Grins and chuckles, is altogether won over.)

(IMAGE: AMANDA AS A GIRL.)

AMANDA

(Coyly smiling, shaking her girlish ringlets)

Well, well, well, so this is Mr. O'Connor. Introductions entirely unnecessary. I've heard so much about you from my boy. I finally said to him, Tom—good gracious!—why don't you bring this paragon to supper? I'd like to meet this nice young man at the warehouse!—Instead of just hearing him sing your praises so much!

78

I don't know why my son is so stand-offish—that's not Southern behavior!

Let's sit down and—I think we could stand a little more air in here! Tom, leave the door open. I felt a nice fresh breeze a moment ago. Where has it gone to?

Mmm, so warm already! And not quite summer, even. We're going to burn up when summer really gets started.

However, we're having—we're having a very light supper. I think light things are better fo' this time of year. The same as light clothes are. Light clothes an' light food are what warm weather calls fo'. You know our blood gets so thick during th' winter—it takes a while fo' us to *adjust* ou'selves! —when the season changes . . .

It's come so quick this year. I wasn't prepared. All of a sudden—heavens! Already summer!—I ran to the trunk an' pulled out this light dress— Terribly old! Historical almost! But feels so good—so good an' co-ol, y' know. . . .

TOM

Mother—

AMANDA

Yes, honey?

TOM

How about—supper?

AMANDA

Honey, you go ask Sister if supper is ready! You know that Sister is in full charge of supper!

Tell her you hungry boys are waiting for it.

(*To* JIM.)

Have you met Laura?

JIM

She—

79

AMANDA

Let you in? Oh, good, you've met already! It's rare for a girl as sweet an' pretty as Laura to be domestic! But Laura is, thank heavens, not only pretty but also very domestic. I'm not at all. I never was a bit. I never could make a thing but angel-food cake. Well, in the South we had so many servants. Gone, gone, gone. All vestige of gracious living! Gone completely! I wasn't prepared for what the future brought me. All of my gentlemen callers were sons of planters and so of course I assumed that I would be married to one and raise my family on a large piece of land with plenty of servants. But man proposes—and woman accepts the proposal!—To vary that old, old saying a little bit—I married no planter! I married a man who worked for the telephone company!— That gallantly smiling gentleman over there! (*Points to the picture*) A telephone man who—fell in love with long-distance!—Now he travels and I don't even know where!— But what am I going on for about my—tribulations? Tell me yours—I hope you don't have any! Tom?

TOM

(*Returning*)

Yes, Mother?

AMANDA

Is supper nearly ready?

TOM

It looks to me like supper is on the table.

AMANDA

Let me look— (*She rises prettily and looks through portieres*) Oh, lovely!—But where is Sister?

80

TOM

Laura is not feeling well and she says that she thinks she'd better not come to the table.

AMANDA

What?—Nonsense!—Laura? Oh, Laura!

LAURA
(*Off stage, faintly*)

Yes, Mother.

AMANDA

You really must come to the table. We won't be seated until you come to the table!

Come in, Mr. O'Connor. You sit over there, and I'll—

Laura? Laura Wingfield!

You're keeping us waiting, honey! We can't say grace until you come to the table!

> (*The back door is pushed weakly open and* LAURA *comes in. She is obviously quite faint, her lips trembling, her eyes wide and staring. She moves unsteadily toward the table.*)
>
> (LEGEND: "TERROR!")
>
> (*Outside a summer storm is coming abruptly. The white curtains billow inward at the windows and there is a sorrowful murmur and deep blue dusk.*)
>
> (LAURA *suddenly stumbles—she catches at a chair with a faint moan.*)

TOM

Laura!

AMANDA

Laura!

> (*There is a clap of thunder.*)

(LEGEND: "AH!")

(*Despairingly*)

Why, Laura, you *are* sick, darling! Tom, help your sister into the living room, dear!

Sit in the living room, Laura—rest on the sofa.

Well!

(*To the gentleman caller.*)

Standing over the hot stove made her ill!—I told her that it was just too warm this evening, but—

(TOM *comes back in.* LAURA *is on the sofa.*)

Is Laura all right now?

TOM

Yes.

AMANDA

What *is* that? Rain? A nice cool rain has come up!

(*She gives the gentleman caller a frightened look.*)

I think we may—have grace—now . . .

(TOM *looks at her stupidly.*)

Tom, honey—you say grace!

TOM

Oh . . .

"For these and all thy mercies—"

(*They bow their heads,* AMANDA *stealing a nervous glance at* JIM. *In the living room* LAURA, *stretched on the sofa, clenches her hand to her lips, to hold back a shuddering sob.*)

God's Holy Name be praised—

THE SCENE DIMS OUT

82

SCENE VII

A Souvenir.

Half an hour later. Dinner is just being finished in the upstage area which is concealed by the drawn portieres.

As the curtain rises LAURA *is still huddled upon the sofa, her feet drawn under her, her head resting on a pale blue pillow, her eyes wide and mysteriously watchful. The new floor lamp with its shade of rose-colored silk gives a soft, becoming light to her face, bringing out the fragile, unearthly prettiness which usually escapes attention. There is a steady murmur of rain, but it is slackening and stops soon after the scene begins; the air outside becomes pale and luminous as the moon breaks out.*

A moment after the curtain rises, the lights in both rooms flicker and go out.

JIM

Hey, there, Mr. Light Bulb!

(AMANDA *laughs nervously.*)

(LEGEND: "SUSPENSION OF A PUBLIC SERVICE.")

AMANDA

Where was Moses when the lights went out? Ha-ha. Do you know the answer to that one, Mr. O'Connor?

JIM

No, Ma'am, what's the answer?

AMANDA

In the dark!

(JIM *laughs appreciatively.*)

Everybody sit still. I'll light the candles. Isn't it lucky we have them on the table? Where's a match? Which of you gentlemen can provide a match?

JIM

Here.

AMANDA

Thank you, sir.

JIM

Not at all, Ma'am!

AMANDA

I guess the fuse has burnt out. Mr. O'Connor, can you tell a burnt-out fuse? I know I can't and Tom is a total loss when it comes to mechanics.

(SOUND: GETTING UP: VOICES RECEDE A LITTLE TO KITCHEN-ETTE.)

Oh, be careful you don't bump into something. We don't want our gentleman caller to break his neck. Now wouldn't that be a fine howdy-do?

JIM

Ha-ha!
Where is the fuse-box?

AMANDA

Right here next to the stove. Can you see anything?

JIM

Just a minute.

AMANDA

Isn't electricity a mysterious thing?
Wasn't it Benjamin Franklin who tied a key to a kite?
We live in such a mysterious universe, don't we? Some

people say that science clears up all the mysteries for us. In my opinion it only creates more!
Have you found it yet?

JIM

No, Ma'am. All these fuses look okay to me.

AMANDA

Tom!

TOM

Yes, Mother?

AMANDA

That light bill I gave you several days ago. The one I told you we got the notices about?

(LEGEND: "HA!")

TOM

Oh.—Yeah.

AMANDA

You didn't neglect to pay it by any chance?

TOM

Why, I—

AMANDA

Didn't! I might have known it!

JIM

Shakespeare probably wrote a poem on that light bill, Mrs. Wingfield.

AMANDA

I might have known better than to trust him with it! There's such a high price for negligence in this world!

JIM

Maybe the poem will win a ten-dollar prize.

AMANDA

We'll just have to spend the remainder of the evening in the nineteenth century, before Mr. Edison made the Mazda lamp!

JIM

Candlelight is my favorite kind of light.

AMANDA

That shows you're romantic! But that's no excuse for Tom. Well, we got through dinner. Very considerate of them to let us get through dinner before they plunged us into ever-lasting darkness, wasn't it, Mr. O'Connor?

JIM

Ha-ha!

AMANDA

Tom, as a penalty for your carelessness you can help me with the dishes.

JIM

Let me give you a hand.

AMANDA

Indeed you will not!

JIM

I ought to be good for something.

AMANDA

Good for something? (*Her tone is rhapsodic.*)
You? Why, Mr. O'Connor, nobody, *nobody's* given me this much entertainment in years—as you have!

JIM

Aw, now, Mrs. Wingfield!

86

AMANDA

I'm not exaggerating, not one bit! But Sister is all by her lonesome. You go keep her company in the parlor!

I'll give you this lovely old candelabrum that used to be on the altar at the church of the Heavenly Rest. It was melted a little out of shape when the church burnt down. Lightning struck it one spring. Gypsy Jones was holding a revival at the time and he intimated that the church was destroyed because the Episcopalians gave card parties.

JIM

Ha-ha.

AMANDA

And how about you coaxing Sister to drink a little wine? I think it would be good for her! Can you carry both at once?

JIM

Sure. I'm Superman!

AMANDA

Now, Thomas, get into this apron!

(*The door of kitchenette swings closed on* AMANDA's *gay laughter; the flickering light approaches the portieres.*)

(LAURA *sits up nervously as he enters. Her speech at first is low and breathless from the almost intolerable strain of being alone with a stranger.*)

(THE LEGEND: "I DON'T SUPPOSE YOU REMEMBER ME AT ALL!")

(*In her first speeches in this scene, before* JIM's *warmth overcomes her paralyzing shyness,* LAURA's *voice is thin and breathless as though she has just run up a steep flight of stairs.*)

87

(JIM's *attitude is gently humorous. In playing this scene it should be stressed that while the incident is apparently unimportant, it is to* LAURA *the climax of her secret life.*)

JIM

Hello, there, Laura.

LAURA

(*Faintly*)

Hello. (*She clears her throat.*)

JIM

How are you feeling now? Better?

LAURA

Yes. Yes, thank you.

JIM

This is for you. A little dandelion wine. (*He extends it toward her with extravagant gallantry.*)

LAURA

Thank you.

JIM

Drink it—but don't get drunk!

(*He laughs heartily.* LAURA *takes the glass uncertainly; laughs shyly.*)

Where shall I set the candles?

LAURA

Oh—oh, anywhere . . .

JIM

How about here on the floor? Any objections?

LAURA

No.

88

JIM

I'll spread a newspaper under to catch the drippings. I like to sit on the floor. Mind if I do?

LAURA

Oh, no.

JIM

Give me a pillow?

LAURA

What?

JIM

A pillow!

LAURA

Oh . . . (*Hands him one quickly.*)

JIM

How about you? Don't you like to sit on the floor?

LAURA

Oh—yes.

JIM

Why don't you, then?

LAURA

I—will.

JIM

Take a pillow! (LAURA *does. Sits on the other side of the candelabrum.* JIM *crosses his legs and smiles engagingly at her*) I can't hardly see you sitting way over there.

LAURA

I can—see you.

JIM

I know, but that's not fair, I'm in the limelight. (LAURA

89

moves her pillow closer) Good! Now I can see you! Comfortable?

LAURA

Yes.

JIM

So am I. Comfortable as a cow! Will you have some gum?

LAURA

No, thank you.

JIM

I think that I will indulge, with your permission. (*Musingly unwraps it and holds it up*) Think of the fortune made by the guy that invented the first piece of chewing gum. Amazing, huh? The Wrigley Building is one of the sights of Chicago.—I saw it summer before last when I went up to the Century of Progress. Did you take in the Century of Progress?

LAURA

No, I didn't.

JIM

Well, it was quite a wonderful exposition. What impressed me most was the Hall of Science. Gives you an idea of what the future will be in America, even more wonderful than the present time is! (*Pause. Smiling at her*) Your brother tells me you're shy. Is that right, Laura?

LAURA

I—don't know.

JIM

I judge you to be an old-fashioned type of girl. Well, I think that's a pretty good type to be. Hope you don't think I'm being too personal—do you?

LAURA

(Hastily, out of embarrassment)
I believe I *will* take a piece of gum, if you—don't mind.
(Clearing her throat) Mr. O'Connor, have you—kept up with
your singing?

JIM

Singing? Me?

LAURA

Yes. I remember what a beautiful voice you had.

JIM

When did you hear me sing?
(VOICE OFF STAGE IN THE PAUSE.)

VOICE

(Off stage)
O blow, ye winds, heigh-ho,
A-roving I will go!
I'm off to my love
With a boxing glove—
Ten thousand miles away!

JIM

You say you've heard me sing?

LAURA

Oh, yes! Yes, very often . . . I—don't suppose—you remember me—at all?

JIM

(Smiling doubtfully)
You know I have an idea I've seen you before. I had that
idea soon as you opened the door. It seemed almost like I was
about to remember your name. But the name that I started

to call you—wasn't a name! And so I stopped myself before
I said it.

LAURA

Wasn't it—Blue Roses?

JIM

(*Springs up. Grinning*)

Blue Roses!—My gosh, yes—Blue Roses!

That's what I had on my tongue when you opened the
door!

Isn't it funny what tricks your memory plays? I didn't con-
nect you with high school somehow or other.

But that's where it was; it was high school. I didn't even
know you were Shakespeare's sister!

Gosh, I'm sorry.

LAURA

I didn't expect you to. You—barely knew me!

JIM

But we did have a speaking acquaintance, huh?

LAURA

Yes, we—spoke to each other.

JIM

When did you recognize me?

LAURA

Oh, right away!

JIM

Soon as I came in the door?

LAURA

When I heard your name I thought it was probably you.

92

I knew that Tom used to know you a little in high school.
So when you came in the door—
   Well, then I was—sure.

JIM

Why didn't you *say* something, then?

LAURA

(*Breathlessly*)
I didn't know what to say, I was—too surprised!

JIM

For goodness' sakes! You know, this sure is funny!

LAURA

Yes! Yes, isn't it, though . .

JIM

Didn't we have a class in something together?

LAURA

Yes, we did.

JIM

What class was that?

LAURA

It was—singing—Chorus!

JIM

Aw!

LAURA

I sat across the aisle from you in the Aud.

JIM

Aw.

LAURA

Mondays, Wednesdays and Fridays.

93

JIM

Now I remember—you always came in late.

LAURA

Yes, it was so hard for me, getting upstairs. I had that brace on my leg—it clumped so loud!

JIM

I never heard any clumping.

LAURA

(*Wincing at the recollection*)
To me it sounded like—thunder!

JIM

Well, well, well, I never even noticed.

LAURA

And everybody was seated before I came in. I had to walk in front of all those people. My seat was in the back row. I had to go clumping all the way up the aisle with everyone watching!

JIM

You shouldn't have been self-conscious.

LAURA

I know, but I was. It was always such a relief when the singing started.

JIM

Aw, yes, I've placed you now! I used to call you Blue Roses. How was it that I got started calling you that?

LAURA

I was out of school a little while with pleurosis. When I came back you asked me what was the matter. I said I had

94

pleurosis—you thought I said Blue Roses. That's what you always called me after that!

JIM

I hope you didn't mind.

LAURA

Oh, no—I liked it. You see, I wasn't acquainted with many —people. . . .

JIM

As I remember you sort of stuck by yourself.

LAURA

I—I—never have had much luck at—making friends.

JIM

I don't see why you wouldn't.

LAURA

Well, I—started out badly.

JIM

You mean being—

LAURA

Yes, it sort of—stood between me—

JIM

You shouldn't have let it!

LAURA

I know, but it did, and—

JIM

You were shy with people!

LAURA

I tried not to be but never could—

JIM

Overcome it?

LAURA

No, I—I never could!

JIM

I guess being shy is something you have to work out of kind of gradually.

LAURA

(*Sorrowfully*)

Yes—I guess it—

JIM

Takes time!

LAURA

Yes—

JIM

People are not so dreadful when you know them. That's what you have to remember! And everybody has problems, not just you, but practically everybody has got some problems. You think of yourself as having the only problems, as being the only one who is disappointed. But just look around you and you will see lots of people as disappointed as you are. For instance, I hoped when I was going to high school that I would be further along at this time, six years later, than I am now— You remember that wonderful write-up I had in *The Torch?*

LAURA

Yes! (*She rises and crosses to table.*)

JIM

It said I was bound to succeed in anything I went into! (LAURA *returns with the annual*) Holy Jeez! *The Torch!* (*He accepts it reverently. They smile across it with mutual won-*

96

der. LAURA *crouches beside him and they begin to turn through it.* LAURA's *shyness is dissolving in his warmth.*)

LAURA

Here you are in *The Pirates of Penzance!*

JIM
(*Wistfully*)

I sang the baritone lead in that operetta.

LAURA
(*Raptly*)

So—*beautifully!*

JIM
(*Protesting*)

Aw—

LAURA

Yes, yes—beautifully—beautifully!

JIM

You heard me?

LAURA

All three times!

JIM

No!

LAURA

Yes!

JIM

All three performances?

LAURA
(*Looking down*)

Yes.

JIM

Why?

97

LAURA

I—wanted to ask you to—autograph my program.

JIM

Why didn't you ask me to?

LAURA

You were always surrounded by your own friends so much that I never had a chance to.

JIM

You should have just—

LAURA

Well, I—thought you might think I was—

JIM

Thought I might think you was—what?

LAURA

Oh—

JIM

(*With reflective relish*)

I was beleaguered by females in those days.

LAURA

You were terribly popular!

JIM

Yeah—

LAURA

You had such a—friendly way—

JIM

I was spoiled in high school.

98

LAURA

Everybody—liked you!

JIM

Including you?

LAURA

I—yes, I—I did, too— (*She gently closes the book in her lap.*)

JIM

Well, well, well!—Give me that program, Laura. (*She hands it to him. He signs it with a flourish*) There you are— better late than never!

LAURA

Oh, I—what a—surprise!

JIM

My signature isn't worth very much right now.
But some day—maybe—it will increase in value!
Being disappointed is one thing and being discouraged is something else. I am disappointed but I am not discouraged.
I'm twenty-three years old.
How old are you?

LAURA

I'll be twenty-four in June.

JIM

That's not old age!

LAURA

No, but—

JIM

You finished high school?

99

LAURA

(*With difficulty*)

I didn't go back.

JIM

You mean you dropped out?

LAURA

I made bad grades in my final examinations. (*She rises and replaces the book and the program. Her voice strained*) How is—Emily Meisenbach getting along?

JIM

Oh, that kraut-head!

LAURA

Why do you call her that?

JIM

That's what she was.

LAURA

You're not still—going with her?

JIM

I never see her.

LAURA

It said in the Personal Section that you were—engaged!

JIM

I know, but I wasn't impressed by that—propaganda!

LAURA

It wasn't—the truth?

JIM

Only in Emily's optimistic opinion!

100

LAURA

Oh—

(LEGEND: "WHAT HAVE YOU DONE SINCE HIGH SCHOOL?")
(JIM *lights a cigarette and leans indolently back on his elbows smiling at* LAURA *with a warmth and charm which lights her inwardly with altar candles. She remains by the table and turns in her hands a piece of glass to cover her tumult.*)

JIM
(*After several reflective puffs on a cigarette*)
What have you done since high school? (*She seems not to hear him*) Huh? (LAURA *looks up*) I said what have you done since high school, Laura?

LAURA

Nothing much.

JIM
You must have been doing something these six long years.

LAURA

Yes.

JIM
Well, then, such as what?

LAURA
I took a business course at business college—

JIM
How did that work out?

LAURA
Well, not very—well—I had to drop out, it gave me—indigestion—

(JIM *laughs gently.*)

JIM

What are you doing now?

LAURA

I don't do anything—much. Oh, please don't think I sit around doing nothing! My glass collection takes up a good deal of time. Glass is something you have to take good care of.

JIM

What did you say—about glass?

LAURA

Collection I said—I have one— (*She clears her throat and turns away again, acutely shy.*)

JIM

(*Abruptly*)

You know what I judge to be the trouble with you?

Inferiority complex! Know what that is? That's what they call it when someone low-rates himself!

I understand it because I had it, too. Although my case was not so aggravated as yours seems to be. I had it until I took up public speaking, developed my voice, and learned that I had an aptitude for science. Before that time I never thought of myself as being outstanding in any way whatsoever!

Now I've never made a regular study of it, but I have a friend who says I can analyze people better than doctors that make a profession of it. I don't claim that to be necessarily true, but I can sure guess a person's psychology, Laura! (*Takes out his gum*) Excuse me, Laura. I always take it out when the flavor is gone. I'll use this scrap of paper to wrap it in. I know how it is to get it stuck on a shoe.

Yep—that's what I judge to be your principal trouble. A

lack of confidence in yourself as a person. You don't have the proper amount of faith in yourself. I'm basing that fact on a number of your remarks and also on certain observations I've made. For instance that clumping you thought was so awful in high school. You say that you even dreaded to walk into class. You see what you did? You dropped out of school, you gave up an education because of a clump, which as far as I know was practically non-existent! A little physical defect is what you have. Hardly noticeable even! Magnified thousands of times by imagination!

You know what my strong advice to you is? Think of yourself as *superior* in some way!

LAURA

In what way would I think?

JIM

Why, man alive, Laura! Just look about you a little. What do you see? A world full of common people! All of 'em born and all of 'em going to die!

Which of them has one-tenth of your good points! Or mine! Or anyone else's, as far as that goes—Gosh!

Everybody excels in some one thing. Some in many!

(*Unconsciously glances at himself in the mirror.*)

All you've got to do is discover in *what!*

Take me, for instance.

(*He adjusts his tie at the mirror.*)

My interest happens to lie in electro-dynamics. I'm taking a course in radio engineering at night school, Laura, on top of a fairly responsible job at the warehouse. I'm taking that course and studying public speaking.

LAURA

Ohhhh.

JIM

Because I believe in the future of television!
(*Turning back to her.*)
I wish to be ready to go up right along with it. Therefore
I'm planning to get in on the ground floor. In fact I've al-
ready made the right connections and all that remains is for
the industry itself to get under way! Full steam—
(*His eyes are starry.*)
Knowledge—Zzzzzp! Money—Zzzzzzp!—Power!
That's the cycle democracy is built on!
(*His attitude is convincingly dynamic.* LAURA *stares at
him, even her shyness eclipsed in her absolute wonder.
He suddenly grins.*)
I guess you think I think a lot of myself!

LAURA

No—o-o-o, I—

JIM

Now how about you? Isn't there something you take more
interest in than anything else?

LAURA

Well, I do—as I said—have my—glass collection—
(*A peal of girlish laughter from the kitchen.*)

JIM

I'm not right sure I know what you're talking about.
What kind of glass is it?

LAURA

Little articles of it, they're ornaments mostly!
Most of them are little animals made out of glass, the tiniest

104

little animals in the world. Mother calls them a glass menagerie!

Here's an example of one, if you'd like to see it!

This one is one of the oldest. It's nearly thirteen.

(MUSIC: "THE GLASS MENAGERIE.")

(*He stretches out his hand.*)

Oh, be careful—if you breathe, it breaks!

JIM

I'd better not take it. I'm pretty clumsy with things.

LAURA

Go on, I trust you with him!

(*Places it in his palm*)

There now—you're holding him gently!

Hold him over the light, he loves the light! You see how the light shines through him?

JIM

It sure does shine!

LAURA

I shouldn't be partial, but he is my favorite one.

JIM

What kind of a thing is this one supposed to be?

LAURA

Haven't you noticed the single horn on his forehead?

JIM

A unicorn, huh?

LAURA

Mmm-hmmm!

JIM

Unicorns, aren't they extinct in the modern world?

LAURA

I know!

JIM

Poor little fellow, he must feel sort of lonesome.

LAURA

(*Smiling*)

Well, if he does he doesn't complain about it. He stays on a shelf with some horses that don't have horns and all of them seem to get along nicely together.

JIM

How do you know?

LAURA

(*Lightly*)

I haven't heard any arguments among them!

JIM

(*Grinning*)

No arguments, huh? Well, that's a pretty good sign! Where shall I set him?

LAURA

Put him on the table. They all like a change of scenery once in a while!

JIM

(*Stretching*)

Well, well, well, well—
Look how big my shadow is when I stretch!

LAURA

Oh, oh, yes—it stretches across the ceiling!

106

JIM

(Crossing to door)

I think it's stopped raining. *(Opens fire-escape door)*
Where does the music come from?

LAURA

From the Paradise Dance Hall across the alley.

JIM

How about cutting the rug a little, Miss Wingfield?

LAURA

Oh, I—

JIM

Or is your program filled up? Let me have a look at it.
(Grasps imaginary card) Why, every dance is taken! I'll just
have to scratch some out. (WALTZ MUSIC: "LA GOLONDRINA")
Ahhh, a waltz! *(He executes some sweeping turns by himself then holds his arms toward* LAURA.)

LAURA

(Breathlessly)

I—can't dance!

JIM

There you go, that inferiority stuff!

LAURA

I've never danced in my life!

JIM

Come on, try!

LAURA

Oh, but I'd step on you!

JIM

I'm not made out of glass.

LAURA

How—how—how do we start?

JIM

Just leave it to me. You hold your arms out a little.

LAURA

Like this?

JIM

A little bit higher. Right. Now don't tighten up, that's the main thing about it—relax.

LAURA

(*Laughing breathlessly*)

It's hard not to.

JIM

Okay.

LAURA

I'm afraid you can't budge me.

JIM

What do you bet I can't? (*He swings her into motion.*)

LAURA

Goodness, yes, you can!

JIM

Let yourself go, now, Laura, just let yourself go.

LAURA

I'm—

JIM

Come on!

LAURA

Trying!

108

JIM

Not so stiff— Easy does it!

LAURA

I know but I'm—

JIM

Loosen th' backbone! There now, that's a lot better.

LAURA

Am I?

JIM

Lots, lots better! (*He moves her about the room in a clumsy waltz.*)

LAURA

Oh, my!

JIM

Ha-ha!

LAURA

Oh, my goodness!

JIM

Ha-ha-ha! (*They suddenly bump into the table.* JIM *stops*) What did we hit on?

LAURA

Table.

JIM

Did something fall off it? I think—

LAURA

Yes.

JIM

I hope that it wasn't the little glass horse with the horn!

LAURA

Yes.

JIM

Aw, aw, aw. Is it broken?

LAURA

Now it is just like all the other horses.

JIM

It's lost its—

LAURA

Horn!
It doesn't matter. Maybe it's a blessing in disguise.

JIM

You'll never forgive me. I bet that that was your favorite piece of glass.

LAURA

I don't have favorites much. It's no tragedy, Freckles. Glass breaks so easily. No matter how careful you are. The traffic jars the shelves and things fall off them.

JIM

Still I'm awfully sorry that I was the cause.

LAURA

(*Smiling*)

I'll just imagine he had an operation.
The horn was removed to make him feel less—freakish!
(*They both laugh.*)
Now he will feel more at home with the other horses, the ones that don't have horns. . .

JIM

Ha-ha, that's very funny!
(*Suddenly serious.*)
I'm glad to see that you have a sense of humor.

110

You know—you're—well—very different!
Surprisingly different from anyone else I know!
  (*His voice becomes soft and hesitant with a genuine feeling.*)
Do you mind me telling you that?
  (LAURA *is abashed beyond speech.*)
I mean it in a nice way . . .
  (LAURA *nods shyly, looking away.*)
You make me feel sort of—I don't know how to put it!
I'm usually pretty good at expressing things, but—
This is something that I don't know how to say!
  (LAURA *touches her throat and clears it—turns the broken unicorn in her hands.*)
  (*Even softer.*)
Has anyone ever told you that you were pretty?
  (PAUSE: MUSIC.)
  (LAURA *looks up slowly, with wonder, and shakes her head.*)
Well, you are! In a very different way from anyone else.
And all the nicer because of the difference, too.
  (*His voice becomes low and husky.* LAURA *turns away, nearly faint with the novelty of her emotions.*)
I wish that you were my sister. I'd teach you to have some confidence in yourself. The different people are not like other people, but being different is nothing to be ashamed of. Because other people are not such wonderful people. They're one hundred times one thousand. You're one times one! They walk all over the earth. You just stay here. They're common as—weeds, but—you—well, you're—*Blue Roses!*
  (IMAGE ON SCREEN: BLUE ROSES.)
  (MUSIC CHANGES.)

LAURA

But blue is wrong for—roses . . .

JIM

It's right for you!—You're—pretty!

LAURA

In what respect am I pretty?

JIM

In all respects—believe me! Your eyes—your hair—are
pretty! Your hands are pretty!

(*He catches hold of her hand.*)

You think I'm making this up because I'm invited to dinner and have to be nice. Oh, I could do that! I could put on
an act for you, Laura, and say lots of things without being
very sincere. But this time I am. I'm talking to you sincerely.
I happened to notice you had this inferiority complex that
keeps you from feeling comfortable with people. Somebody
needs to build your confidence up and make you proud instead of shy and turning away and—blushing—

Somebody—ought to—

Ought to—*kiss* you, Laura!

(*His hand slips slowly up her arm to her shoulder.*)

(MUSIC SWELLS TUMULTUOUSLY.)

(*He suddenly turns her about and kisses her on the
lips.*)

(*When he releases her,* LAURA *sinks on the sofa with a
bright, dazed look.*)

(JIM *backs away and fishes in his pocket for a cigarette.*)

(LEGEND ON SCREEN: "SOUVENIR.")

Stumble-john!

(*He lights the cigarette, avoiding her look.*)

(*There is a peal of girlish laughter from* AMANDA *in the kitchen.*)

(LAURA *slowly raises and opens her hand. It still contains the little broken glass animal. She looks at it with a tender, bewildered expression.*)

Stumble-john!

I shouldn't have done that— That was way off the beam. You don't smoke, do you?

(*She looks up, smiling, not hearing the question.*)

(*He sits beside her a little gingerly. She looks at him speechlessly—waiting.*)

(*He coughs decorously and moves a little farther aside as he considers the situation and senses her feelings, dimly, with perturbation.*)

(*Gently.*)

Would you—care for a—mint?

(*She doesn't seem to hear him but her look grows brighter even.*)

Peppermint—Life-Saver?

My pocket's a regular drug store—wherever I go . . .

(*He pops a mint in his mouth. Then gulps and decides to make a clean breast of it. He speaks slowly and gingerly.*)

Laura, you know, if I had a sister like you, I'd do the same thing as Tom. I'd bring out fellows and—introduce her to them. The right type of boys of a type to—appreciate her.

Only—well—he made a mistake about me.

Maybe I've got no call to be saying this. That may not have been the idea in having me over. But what if it was?

There's nothing wrong about that. The only trouble is that in my case—I'm not in a situation to—do the right thing.

I can't take down your number and say I'll phone.
I can't call up next week and—ask for a date.
I thought I had better explain the situation in case you—
misunderstood it and—hurt your feelings. . . .

> (*Pause.*)
> (*Slowly, very slowly,* LAURA's *look changes, her eyes
> returning slowly from his to the ornament in her
> palm.*)
> (AMANDA *utters another gay laugh in the kitchen.*)

LAURA
(Faintly)

You—won't—call again?

JIM

No, Laura, I can't.

> (*He rises from the sofa.*)

As I was just explaining, I've—got strings on me.
Laura, I've—been going steady!

I go out all of the time with a girl named Betty. She's a
home-girl like you, and Catholic, and Irish, and in a great
many ways we—get along fine.

I met her last summer on a moonlight boat trip up the river
to Alton, on the *Majestic*.

Well—right away from the start it was—love!

> (LEGEND: LOVE!)
> (LAURA *sways slightly forward and grips the arm of the
> sofa. He fails to notice, now enrapt in his own com-
> fortable being.*)

Being in love has made a new man of me!

> (*Leaning stiffly forward, clutching the arm of the sofa,*
> LAURA *struggles visibly with her storm. But* JIM *is
> oblivious, she is a long way off.*)

The power of love is really pretty tremendous!

Love is something that—changes the whole world, Laura!

   (*The storm abates a little and* LAURA *leans back. He notices her again.*)

It happened that Betty's aunt took sick, she got a wire and had to go to Centralia. So Tom—when he asked me to dinner—I naturally just accepted the invitation, not knowing that you—that he—that I—

   (*He stops awkwardly.*)

Huh—I'm a stumble-john!

   (*He flops back on the sofa.*)

   (*The holy candles in the altar of* LAURA*'s face have been snuffed out. There is a look of almost infinite desolation.*)

   (JIM *glances at her uneasily.*)

I wish that you would—say something. (*She bites her lip which was trembling and then bravely smiles. She opens her hand again on the broken glass ornament. Then she gently takes his hand and raises it level with her own. She carefully places the unicorn in the palm of his hand, then pushes his fingers closed upon it*) What are you—doing that for? You want me to have him?—Laura? (*She nods*) What for?

LAURA

A—souvenir . . .

   (*She rises unsteadily and crouches beside the victrola to wind it up.*)

   (LEGEND ON SCREEN: "THINGS HAVE A WAY OF TURNING OUT SO BADLY!")

   (OR IMAGE: "GENTLEMAN CALLER WAVING GOOD-BYE!—GAILY.")

   (*At this moment* AMANDA *rushes brightly back in the*

115

front room. She bears a pitcher of fruit punch in an
old-fashioned cut-glass pitcher and a plate of macaroons.
The plate has a gold border and poppies painted on it.)

AMANDA

Well, well, well! Isn't the air delightful after the shower?
I've made you children a little liquid refreshment.
(*Turns gaily to the gentleman caller*)
Jim, do you know that song about lemonade?
"Lemonade, lemonade
    Made in the shade and stirred with a spade—
    Good enough for any old maid!"

JIM
(*Uneasily*)
Ha-ha! No—I never heard it.

AMANDA

Why, Laura! You look so serious!

JIM

We were having a serious conversation.

AMANDA

Good! Now you're better acquainted!

JIM
(*Uncertainly*)
Ha-ha! Yes.

AMANDA

You modern young people are much more serious-minded
than my generation. I was so gay as a girl!

JIM

You haven't changed, Mrs. Wingfield.

116

AMANDA

Tonight I'm rejuvenated! The gaiety of the occasion, Mr.
O'Connor!

(*She tosses her head with a pearl of laughter. Spills
lemonade.*)

Oooo! I'm baptizing myself!

JIM

Here—let me—

AMANDA

(*Setting the pitcher down*)

There now. I discovered we had some maraschino cherries.
I dumped them in, juice and all!

JIM

You shouldn't have gone to that trouble, Mrs. Wingfield.

AMANDA

Trouble, trouble? Why, it was loads of fun!

Didn't you hear me cutting up in the kitchen? I bet your
ears were burning! I told Tom how outdone with him I was
for keeping you to himself so long a time! He should have
brought you over much, much sooner! Well, now that you've
found your way, I want you to be a very frequent caller! Not
just occasional but all the time.

Oh, we're going to have a lot of gay times together! I see
them coming!

Mmm, just breathe that air! So fresh, and the moon's so
pretty!

I'll skip back out—I know where my place is when young
folks are having a—serious conversation!

117

JIM

Oh, don't go out, Mrs. Wingfield. The fact of the matter is I've got to be going.

AMANDA

Going, now? You're joking! Why, it's only the shank of the evening, Mr. O'Connor!

JIM

Well, you know how it is.

AMANDA

You mean you're a young workingman and have to keep workingmen's hours. We'll let you off early tonight. But only on the condition that next time you stay later.

What's the best night for you? Isn't Saturday night the best night for you workingmen?

JIM

I have a couple of time-clocks to punch, Mrs. Wingfield. One at morning, another one at night!

AMANDA

My, but you *are* ambitious! You work at night, too?

JIM

No, Ma'am, not work but—Betty! (*He crosses deliberately to pick up his hat. The band at the Paradise Dance Hall goes into a tender waltz.*)

AMANDA

Betty? Betty? Who's—Betty!
(*There is an ominous cracking sound in the sky.*)

JIM

Oh, just a girl. The girl I go steady with! (*He smiles charmingly. The sky falls.*)
  (LEGEND: "THE SKY FALLS.")

AMANDA

(*A long-drawn exhalation*)
Ohhhh . . . Is it a serious romance, Mr. O'Connor?

JIM

We're going to be married the second Sunday in June.

AMANDA

Ohhhh—how nice!
Tom didn't mention that you were engaged to be married.

JIM

The cat's not out of the bag at the warehouse yet.
You know how they are. They call you Romeo and stuff like that.
  (*He stops at the oval mirror to put on his hat. He carefully shapes the brim and the crown to give a discreetly dashing effect.*)
It's been a wonderful evening, Mrs. Wingfield. I guess this is what they mean by Southern hospitality.

AMANDA

It really wasn't anything at all.

JIM

I hope it don't seem like I'm rushing off. But I promised Betty I'd pick her up at the Wabash depot, an' by the time I get my jalopy down there her train'll be in. Some women are pretty upset if you keep 'em waiting.

AMANDA

Yes, I know— The tyranny of women!
(Extends her hand.)
Good-bye, Mr. O'Connor.
I wish you luck—and happiness—and success! All three of them, and so does Laura!—Don't you, Laura?

LAURA

Yes!

JIM

(Taking her hand)
Good-bye, Laura. I'm certainly going to treasure that souvenir. And don't you forget the good advice I gave you.
(Raises his voice to a cheery shout.)
So long, Shakespeare!
Thanks again, ladies— Good night!
(He grins and ducks jauntily out.)
(Still bravely grimacing, AMANDA *closes the door on the gentleman caller. Then she turns back to the room with a puzzled expression. She and* LAURA *don't dare to face each other.* LAURA *crouches beside the victrola to wind it.)*

AMANDA

(Faintly)
Things have a way of turning out so badly.
I don't believe that I would play the victrola.
Well, well—well—
Our gentleman caller was engaged to be married!
Tom!

TOM

(From back)
Yes, Mother?

THE GLASS MENAGERIE

AMANDA

Come in here a minute. I want to tell you something awfully funny.

TOM

(*Enters with macaroon and a glass of the lemonade*)
Has the gentleman caller gotten away already?

AMANDA

The gentleman caller has made an early departure.
What a wonderful joke you played on us!

TOM

How do you mean?

AMANDA

You didn't mention that he was engaged to be married.

TOM

Jim? Engaged?

AMANDA

That's what he just informed us.

TOM

I'll be jiggered! I didn't know about that.

AMANDA

That seems very peculiar.

TOM

What's peculiar about it?

AMANDA

Didn't you call him your best friend down at the warehouse?

TOM

He is, but how did I know?

AMANDA

It seems extremely peculiar that you wouldn't know your best friend was going to be married!

TOM

The warehouse is where I work, not where I know things about people!

AMANDA

You don't know things anywhere! You live in a dream; you manufacture illusions!
(*He crosses to door.*)
Where are you going?

TOM

I'm going to the movies.

AMANDA

That's right, now that you've had us make such fools of ourselves. The effort, the preparations, all the expense! The new floor lamp, the rug, the clothes for Laura! All for what? To entertain some other girl's fiancé!

Go to the movies, go! Don't think about us, a mother deserted, an unmarried sister who's crippled and has no job! Don't let anything interfere with your selfish pleasure! Just go, go, go—to the movies!

TOM

All right, I will! The more you shout about my selfishness to me the quicker I'll go, and I won't go to the movies!

AMANDA

Go, then! Then go to the moon—you selfish dreamer!
(TOM *smashes his glass on the floor. He plunges out on the fire-escape, slamming the door.* LAURA *screams— cut by door.*)

(*Dance-hall music up.* TOM *goes to the rail and grips it desperately, lifting his face in the chill white moonlight penetrating the narrow abyss of the alley.*)

(LEGEND ON SCREEN: "AND SO GOOD-BYE . . .")

(TOM's *closing speech is timed with the interior pantomime. The interior scene is played as though viewed through soundproof glass.* AMANDA *appears to be making a comforting speech to* LAURA *who is huddled upon the sofa. Now that we cannot hear the mother's speech, her silliness is gone and she has dignity and tragic beauty.* LAURA's *dark hair hides her face until at the end of the speech she lifts it to smile at her mother.* AMANDA's *gestures are slow and graceful, almost dancelike, as she comforts the daughter. At the end of her speech she glances a moment at the father's picture— then withdraws through the portieres. At close of* TOM's *speech,* LAURA *blows out the candles, ending the play.*)

TOM

I didn't go to the moon, I went much further—for time is the longest distance between two places—

Not long after that I was fired for writing a poem on the lid of a shoe-box.

I left Saint Louis. I descended the steps of this fire-escape for a last time and followed, from then on, in my father's footsteps, attempting to find in motion what was lost in space—

I traveled around a great deal. The cities swept about me like dead leaves, leaves that were brightly colored but torn away from the branches.

I would have stopped, but I was pursued by something. It always came upon me unawares, taking me altogether by surprise. Perhaps it was a familiar bit of music. Perhaps it was only a piece of transparent glass—

Perhaps I am walking along a street at night, in some strange city, before I have found companions. I pass the lighted window of a shop where perfume is sold. The window is filled with pieces of colored glass, tiny transparent bottles in delicate colors, like bits of a shattered rainbow.

Then all at once my sister touches my shoulder. I turn around and look into her eyes . . .

Oh, Laura, Laura, I tried to leave you behind me, but I am more faithful than I intended to be!

I reach for a cigarette, I cross the street, I run into the movies or a bar, I buy a drink, I speak to the nearest stranger —anything that can blow your candles out!

(LAURA *bends over the candles.*)

—for nowadays the world is lit by lightning! Blow out your candles, Laura—and so good-bye. . . .

(*She blows the candles out.*)

THE SCENE DISSOLVES